Simon,

With all good wishes for the future.

From Frank, Alison, Dougie & Andrew.

(Willoughby.)

The OUTDOOR POCKET BIBLE

The OUTDOOR POCKET BIBLE

EVERY OUTDOOR RULE OF THUMB
at your fingertips

PAUL JENNER &
CHRISTINE SMITH

EDITOR Roni Jay

WHITE
LADDER
PRESS
new tricks for old dogs

The Outdoor Pocket Bible

This edition first published in Great Britain 2008 by

Crimson Publishing, a division of Crimson Business Ltd
Westminster House
Kew Road
Richmond
Surrey
TW9 2ND

ISBN 978 1 905410 47 7

Designed and typeset by Julie Martin Ltd
Cover design by Julie Martin Ltd
Printed and bound by L.E.G.O. S.p.A., Italy

Contents

INTRODUCTION

You're strolling along and you see a track in the mud. Which animal made it? Or you glimpse a wild creature through the trees. Is it a roe deer or a fallow deer? Or you're lost and can't find your place on the map. Where are you? Darkness is falling and you need to make a shelter. But how? A storm is brewing and there's lightning in the distance. Where's the safest place to be? The storm is over and the moon is bright enough to walk by but which is the way home? You need to cross a sandbank but what will the tide be doing?

These are just a few of the many questions answered by *The Outdoor Pocket Bible*.

The outdoors is a wonderful place to be. And since the introduction of the Countryside and Rights of Way (CRoW) Act, a great deal more of it is now open to you than before. To check the full details of where you can now walk see: **www.countryside access.gov.uk**

However, CRoW does *not* give you permission to:

- Light fires
- Damage plant or animal life
- Hold organised games
- Bathe in non-tidal waters
- Walk over crops or through private gardens

○ Allow your dog near livestock or off the lead between 1 March and 31 July

And while we're at it we may as well remind you that the Countryside Code requires you to:

○ Leave gates and property as you find them
○ Protect plants and animals
○ Take your litter home
○ Keep dogs under close control
○ Consider other people
○ Be safe, plan ahead and follow signs

WILD FOOD

It's incredibly satisfying to harvest wild food when you're out walking but don't rely on it to provide you with a meal. If you can find enough to make a serious contribution you'll be doing well.

The following notes are intended as a reminder to help you with identification. If you're not already familiar with the plants you'll need to buy a good field guide.

✳ MUSHROOMS ✳

What's the difference between mushrooms and toadstools? In fact, there is no difference scientifically but the word 'mushroom' tends to be used for edible species and the word 'toadstool' for poisonous ones.

SAFETY RULES FOR COLLECTING MUSHROOMS TO EAT 🦯

- Don't eat any wild mushroom you're not 100% sure of – it just isn't worth the risk.
- Don't eat a mixed plate of wild mushrooms – if somebody does get ill it helps to know exactly which mushroom was the cause.
- Don't eat a large quantity of any mushroom you're not used to – it may not be poisonous but it may still upset you.

Rule of thumb —O

Don't eat any mushroom with a volva or sheath (see below) –
not all mushrooms with volvas are poisonous but the deadliest
toadstools in Britain (the Death Cap and the Destroying Angel)
have volvas.

HOW TO PICK MUSHROOMS

Unless otherwise stated, mushrooms should be collected with a
gentle, twisting motion that avoids damaging the mycelium (the
part of the fungus in the ground) but at the same time liberates the
entire stem and any volva as an aid to identification.

If you're lucky enough to be able to gather some along the way:

○ Don't put them into a plastic bag or a jacket pocket; they'll
deteriorate very quickly.

Instead, clean any mud off the stems, put the mushrooms into a
string bag (or improvise something with, say, a silk scarf) and attach
it firmly to the outside of your backpack.

If you can already see that a mushroom is unlikely to be edible
don't pick it just out of curiosity – you'll be destroying the fruiting,
reproductive body for nothing. And don't be tempted to pick more
than you can eat fairly swiftly.

HOW TO COOK MUSHROOMS

See the next chapter.

Identifying characteristics of mushrooms

Cap – the colour, shape and size of the cap are among the key
identifying features.

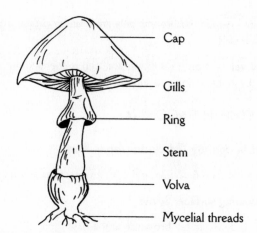

Cap

Gills

Ring

Stem

Volva

Mycelial threads

Spore-bearing surface – the underside of the cap releases spores which can be likened to seeds. There are four main kinds of spore-bearing surfaces and they're quite distinct:
  - Pores – masses of tiny holes or tubes giving the appearance of a sponge.
  - Gills – a radial pattern of hundreds of separate, thin walls running from the stem to the edge of the cap.
  - Folds – at a glance, folds may look like gills but upon investigation there's no depth to the cracks between them.
  - Spines – individual bristles like those on a brush or like the spines of a hedgehog.

Stem – the column on which the cap is supported.

Volva (sheath) – an egg-shaped bag right at the base from which the stems of certain mushrooms emerge.

Ring – as the name suggests, a ring of extra flesh part way up the stem of some varieties; in a few species it can actually be moved up and down.

Situation – certain mushrooms only grow under certain trees or on certain soils.

Time of year – most mushrooms are seen in the autumn but a few occur in the spring and summer.

SOME EDIBLE MUSHROOMS 🍄

Wood hedgehog (Hydnum repandum)

Cap: Smooth and buff-coloured with a wavy incurved ring.

Spore-bearing surface: Spines.

Stem: Mostly white but brownish at the base.

Volva: No.

Ring: No.

Situation: Usually broad-leaved woodland.

Size: 3-8cm high x 5-10cm across.

Time of year: Autumn.

Could be confused with: Unlikely to be confused with anything else.

Chanterelle (Cantharellus cibarius)

Cap: Egg-yellow and slightly funnel-shaped with wavy rim.

Spore-bearing surface: Folds.

Stem: Short and also egg-yellow.

Volva: No.

Ring: No.

Situation: In groups under beech, oak, birch and conifers.

Size: 4-7cm high x 3-11cm across.

Time of year: Autumn.

Could be confused with: False Chanterelle (*Hygrophoropsis aurantiaca*) but this has gills not folds.

Lactarius deliciosus

Cap: Orange with darker-orange bands and slightly funnel-shaped.

Spore-bearing surface: Orange-yellow gills.

Stem: Orange with greenish spots when older; if you cut it it's carrot-coloured all through and produces orange juice.

Volva: No.

Ring: No.

Situation: Usually under pine trees.

Size: 3-5cm high x 4-10cm across.

Time of year: Summer/autumn.

Could be confused with: *Lactarius torminosus* which has a pinky cap with a hairy edge or *Lactarius quietus* which has a reddy-brown cap and grows under oak trees, neither of which has orange juice.

Parasol mushroom (*Lepiota procera*)

Cap: Brown at first but as it opens fully it transforms into brown scales on a paler background.

Spore-bearing surface: White or creamy gills.

Stem: Tall and slender with darker brown streaks on a paler background.

Volva: No.

Ring: Yes. It's whitish and can be slid up and down.

Situation: Roadsides and the edges of woods.

Size: Extremely large. 15-40cm tall and 10-30cm across.

Time of year: Summer/autumn.

Could be confused with: The Shaggy Parasol (*Lepiota rhacodes*) which is also edible, see below; and the Stinking Parasol (*Lepiota cristata*) which is not edible but which is *much* smaller (cap 2-7cm).

Shaggy Parasol (Lepiota rhacodes)

Cap: Brown at first but as it opens fully it transforms into brown scales on a paler background.

Spore-bearing surface: White or creamy gills.

Stem: Not as tall as the Parasol Mushroom (above) and thicker and more evenly coloured fawn.

Volva: No.

Ring: Yes. It's whitish and can be slid up and down.

Situation: Rich soils in the shade.

Size: Quite large. 10-30cm tall and 8-13cm across.

Time of year: Autumn.

Could be confused with: The Parasol Mushroom (*Lepiota procera*) which is also edible, see above; and the Stinking Parasol

(*Lepiota cristata*) which is not edible but which is *much* smaller (cap 2-7cm).

Penny Bun or Cep (Boletus edulis)

Cap: Smooth and brown, just like a 'penny bun'.

Spore-bearing surface: Tubes which are white or dirty yellow.

Stem: Extremely thick and pale fawn.

Volva: No.

Ring: No.

Situation: Under all kinds of trees.

Size: 5-15cm high x 5-20cm across.

Time of year: Autumn.

Could be confused with: Other members of the same species which are *mostly* but not all edible.

Rule of thumb ─○

There is a number of species related to the Cep. In Britain, any similar mushroom with a tubular spore-bearing surface is safe to eat *if cooked* provided it *isn't tinged red or purple*. Some make better eating than others but at least you can be confident you're not going to die.

Morel (Morchella esculenta)

Cap: Extraordinary deeply indented pale-brown honeycomb shaped like an elongated dome.

Spore-bearing surface: The spores are in bags known as asci.

Stem: Hollow, white and brittle.

Volva: No.

Ring: No.

Situation: Broad-leaved woods or grassland.

Size: 8-20cm high x 3-5cm across.

Time of year: Spring.

Could be confused with: *Morchella elata* which is also edible (see below) and *Gyromitra esculenta* which resembles a brown brain and seems to be edible *if first dried* but is best avoided.

Morel (Morchella elata)

Cap: Extraordinary deeply indented dark-brown honeycomb shaped like a missile.

Spore-bearing surface: The spores are in bags known as asci.

Stem: Hollow, white and brittle.

Volva: No.

Ring: No.

Situation: Under conifers and on chalky soils.

Size: 5-10cm high x 1-3cm across.

Time of year: Spring.

Could be confused with: *Morchella esculenta* which is also edible (see above) and *Gyromitra esculenta* which resembles a brown brain and seems to be edible *if first dried* but is best avoided.

Field mushroom (Agaricus campestris)

Cap: White becoming slightly brown and scaly at the centre with age.

Spore-bearing surface: Tightly-packed gills which are pinkish at first turning brown with age.

Stem: White and solid.

Volva: No.

Ring: Apparent when young but disappears with age.

Situation: Grassland. May occur in rings.

Size: 4-7cm high x 5-10cm across.

Time of year: Autumn.

Could be confused with: The Horse Mushroom (*Agaricus arvensis*) which is also edible (see below); the Wood Mushroom (*Agaricus silvicola*) which is also edible (see below) and the Yellow-Staining Mushroom (*Agaricus xanthodermus*) which is poisonous. The Yellow-Staining Mushroom can be distinguished by the fact that if you cut through the base of the stem *it immediately turns a brilliant yellow*. Neither the Field Mushroom nor the Horse Mushroom shows any tendency to yellowing although the Wood Mushroom does slightly.

Horse mushroom (Agaricus arvensis)

Cap: White dome.

Spore-bearing surface: Tightly-packed gills which are white at first turning grey then brown with age.

Stem: White.

Volva: No.

Ring: Yes.

Situation: Near stables and cowsheds.

Size: 8-13cm high x 7-15cm across.

Time of year: Autumn.

Could be confused with: The Field Mushroom (*Agaricus campestris*) which is also edible (see above); the Wood Mushroom (*Agaricus silvicola*) which is also edible (see below) and the Yellow-Staining Mushroom (*Agaricus xanthodermus*) which is poisonous. The Yellow-Staining Mushroom can be distinguished by the fact that if you cut through the base of the stem *it immediately turns a brilliant yellow*. Neither the Field Mushroom nor the Horse Mushroom shows any tendency to yellowing although the Wood Mushroom does slightly.

Wood mushroom (Agaricus silvicola)

Cap: White.

Spore-bearing surface: Tightly-packed brown gills.

Stem: White.

Volva: No.

Ring: Yes.

Situation: Woodland, usually under conifers.

Size: 6-8cm high x 5-8cm across.

Time of year: Autumn.

Could be confused with: The Field Mushroom (*Agaricus campestris*) which is also edible (see above); the Horse Mushroom (*Agaricus arvensis*) which is also edible (see above) and the Yellow-Staining Mushroom (*Agaricus xanthodermus*) which is poisonous. The Yellow-Staining Mushroom can be distinguished by the fact that if you cut through the base of the stem *it immediately turns a brilliant yellow*. Neither the Field Mushroom nor the Horse Mushroom shows any tendency to yellowing although the Wood Mushroom does slightly.

Oyster mushroom (Pleurotus ostreatus)

Cap: Deep bluish-grey and shaped roughly like an oyster.

Spore-bearing surface: Off-white gills.

Stem: A small extension of the gills.

Volva: No.

Ring: No.

Situation: Grows on the dead or dying parts of broad-leaved trees, especially beech and ash, often quite high up.

Size: 2-3cm high x 6-15cm across.

Time of year: All year but most common in autumn.

Could be confused with: Most bracket-style fungi that grow on wood have tubes/pores rather than the Oyster Mushroom's gills, so it's unlikely to be confused with anything else.

❋ SOME TREES AND BUSHES ❋ WITH EDIBLE PARTS

Hawthorn or May (Crataegus monogyna)

Form: Large shrub or small tree with vicious spikes along the branches.

Leaves: Distinctive dark green and deeply lobed.

Other identifying features: The flowers have five white petals (turning pinkish later) which give way to bright red berries known as haws.

What can you eat? The blossoms can be used in an infusion. The leaves have a nutty taste and are good in salads. The berries are also edible. All are said to be good for the heart.

Hazel (Corylus avellana)

Form: Normally grows as a bush with a dense mass of branches growing from the ground, although it can also form a tree.

Leaves: Rounded with a pointed tip and edges that look as if they've been nibbled by a mouse.

Other identifying features: In spring there are long, yellow catkins.

What can you eat? The nuts. They start appearing on the bushes in August but are probably best picked in September. Crack them and eat them as they are or add them to muesli.

Lime (Tilia europaea or Tilia x vulgaris)

Form: Tall tree

Leaves: Large and heart-shaped with a point and notched edges.

Other identifying features: Dark bark with ridges, cracks and sprouting bosses. Clusters of 4-10 yellow-green flowers that open in July.

What can you eat? The young leaves are good in salad. The yellow flowers (June/July) can be dried and used as an infusion.

Sweet chestnut (Castanea sativa)

Form: Large tree with massive branches.

Leaves: Long, narrow and pointed with teeth all around the edges.

Other identifying features: The bark has deep spiral ridges.

What can you eat? Sweet chestnuts are usually at their best in late October and November. Roll the prickly casings underfoot to liberate the nuts. They can be eaten raw but are best cooked (see next chapter).

❋ SOME OTHER PLANTS WITH ❋ EDIBLE PARTS

Blackberry or Bramble (Rubus fruticosus)

Form: This prickly plant with long, curving, purplish-green shoots needs little introduction.

Leaves: Elliptical with a pointed tip and toothed edges.

Other identifying features: The black berries which are composed of shiny 'drupelets'.

What can you eat? The berries – raw, stewed alone or with other fruit, or in pies.

Blackthorn or Sloe (Prunus spinosa)

Form: Dense shrub.

Leaves: Elongated ovals, slightly notched.

Other identifying features: Long, vicious thorns.

What can you eat? The dark blue fruits (green inside) are too acid for most tastes but can be collected in the autumn to flavour gin (pierce the skins and add sugar to taste). The deep pink liqueur will be ready in about two months and the fruits will, by then, be edible, too.

Dandelion (Taraxacum officinale)

Form: Everybody knows the dandelion, the small, yellow-flowered meadow plant.

Leaves: Deeply toothed.

Other identifying features: The flowers turn to round 'fairies' for blowing.

What can you eat? The leaves are very good in salads, especially when young and dressed in olive oil, lemon juice and garlic. For how to cook the roots see the next chapter.

Fat-hen or Wild spinach (Chenopodium album)

Form: Pyramid-shaped plant up to about 3ft (1m) tall.

Leaves: Jagged and somewhat diamond-shaped.

Other identifying features: One of the first plants to appear on waste ground.

What can you eat? The leaves can be cooked just like spinach.

Fennel (Foeniculum vulgare)

Form: Celery-like stalk growing from knee-high to chest-high.

Leaves: Fronds of thin leaves giving a fern-like effect.

Other identifying features: Mustard-yellow blossoms in summer and an unmistakable aniseed smell, especially when the leaves are rubbed or the stalk snapped.

What can you eat? Stalk, leaves, bulb and seeds.

Stinging nettle (Urtica dioica)

Form: Another well-known plant, growing to more than 3ft (1m) high.

Leaves: Heart-shaped and notched.

Other identifying features: The leaves have hairs that sting.

What can you eat? Incredibly, the leaves in springtime can be made into a tasty soup (see next chapter).

Wild strawberry (Fragaria vesca)

Form: Low, creeping plant much like the cultivated variety.

Leaves: Oval, toothed and arranged three per stem.

Other identifying features: Red fruits in summer.

What can you eat? The fruit, which is smaller but often tastier than the cultivated types.

Wood sorrel (Oxalis acetosella)

Form: Small, low plant with reddish stems.

Leaves: Arranged as three heart shapes, all joined together at their pointed ends.

Other identifying features: White, bell-shaped flowers in spring. Likes shade and is often found on the floor of pine forests.

What can you eat? The leaves can be used in soup (see next chapter).

❉ SOME SEASIDE PLANTS ❉ WITH EDIBLE PARTS

Carragheen or Irish moss (Chondrus crispus)

Form: Deep purple fern-like seaweed.

Other identifying features: Grows on rocks on the Atlantic coast.

What can you eat? The fronds can be used to make jelly or blanc-mange (see next chapter).

Laver (Porphyra umbilicalis)

Form: Thin, flat, purple seaweed like the translucent leaves of a red cabbage.

Other identifying features: Grows on rocks on the beach especially on the West coast of Britain.

What can you eat? The fronds make what the Welsh call laver-bread (see next chapter).

Marsh samphire or Glasswort (Salicornia europaea)

Form: It can appear as single shoots or as clumps, anything up to about 1ft (30cm) tall.

Leaves: The green, shiny, jointed stems are effectively the leaves.

Other identifying features: It grows only on salt marshes.

What can you eat? Marsh samphire is one of the few wild plants that can be gathered in sufficient abundance to make a significant contribution to a meal. In the early summer you can just pinch the shoots off above the root and use them in salads. In late summer or early autumn when the shoots are tougher you'll have to pull up the whole plant and cook it as described in the next chapter.

WATER

Rule of thumb

Walking in Britain, work on the basis of *at least* 2.5 litres per person per day.

In hot weather on a steep route you're going to need much more than 2.5 litres a day. Obviously, it's very difficult to shoulder such an amount, especially if there are children in the group who can't carry very much. Make it a rule that you will always:

- Drink as much as you possibly can before you set off.

And, of course, if you're only out for the day you can replenish your body's supplies when you get back.

Even so, to keep your body moving efficiently you need to keep it topped up. A litre per person is a reasonable quantity to take with you for a day out. Unfortunately, it's heavy stuff:

○ One litre (one and three-quarter pints) weighs one kilogram (2.2lb).

So if you're going for more than a day out you can't possibly carry enough and you're going to have to find water along the way.

Don't drink untreated water if it's been collected:

○ Downstream from a town, village, campsite or heavily-used path
○ Where there are cows or sheep
○ Where the water is stagnant or full of weeds

Do collect water at the *outflow* of a lake rather than at the inflow (assuming, of course, there's no pollution of the lake itself). The water will be cleanest in the middle of a lake (if you have any way of getting there).

HOW TO PURIFY WATER 🐾

If necessary, clarify the water by letting it stand for a while or by straining through a cloth and then do one of the following:

○ Add iodine (see the instructions on the bottle or packet for the correct quantity) and leave to stand for 15 minutes.
○ Use a water filter/purifier specially designed for backpacking.
○ Boil vigorously for 10 minutes.

For how to collect water see pages 71–72.

FIRES AND COOKING OUT OF DOORS

A camp fire is a lovely thing. There's nothing like it for drying clothes, for warming you through and cheering you up. But the fire rings left behind are far from beautiful and there are dangers, too.

Always use a camping stove:

- If you don't have the permission of the landowner to light a real fire.
- If there's the slightest chance a real fire might set the country-side alight.
- If you're in an area where there's very little dead wood.
- If you're in an unusually sensitive area.
- If you aren't willing to reinstate the site of a fire as it was when you leave.

Nevertheless, there are occasions a real fire is appropriate and, then, it's a great treat.

HOW TO LIGHT A FIRE

Forget all the stuff about rubbing sticks together. Have with you a commercial firelighter (well wrapped until needed) or a candle stub, plus a lighter and a box of 'lifeboat' matches as a backup – you can buy them in yachtie shops. It may be sissy but it works. (If, for whatever reason, you don't have the necessary items with you, see the chapter on *Survival skills*.)

⦿ Choose bare ground well away from your tent and gear and any vegetation that might catch fire. If you have no choice but to light a fire on grass, dig up a section of turf and set it aside. Light your fire in the hole and, when it's burned away and is cold, replace the turf.

⦿ Create a 'stove' to protect the fire and reflect the heat back by building a little U-shape from logs or rocks. If you intend to cook on the fire you'll also need to construct something from which to hang a cooking pot. For example, you could push two Y-shaped pieces of wood into the ground either side of the fire and place a supporting strut across them.

⦿ Don't light the fire and then begin looking for wood. *Assemble everything before you start.* Have handy an extensive range of dry fuel from tinder through twigs up to wrist-thick logs. If you can't find dry twigs shave a thicker piece of wood but leave the shavings attached – it should end up looking like a Christmas tree.

⦿ Resinous wood (for example, Scots pine) burns easily but ash, beech, birch, hawthorn, hornbeam and oak all make a good fire (see *Identifying What You See*).

⦿ If there's no dry tinder obviously available (pine needles are good) you'll have to make some by shaving a piece of dead wood with a knife – even if it's raining the interior will still be dry. Similarly, if you can't find any larger wood that isn't rain-soaked, split some open. Don't use green (living) wood.

- Set light to your firelighter or candle stub or just the tinder on its own and then *very slowly* add tinder followed by the *tiniest* twigs followed by *fractionally* larger twigs . . . and so on.
- Be *patient*. Don't add larger wood too quickly.

COOKING OUT OF DOORS

Cooking over a camp fire (or stove) in the wilderness is very different from cooking on a hob at an organised campsite with the car right next to you and vastly different from cooking at home. You don't have a nice, clean, flat preparation area, or fancy tools and machines, or an oven (although, as you'll see in *Survival skills*, it is possible to improvise something) or even a choice of saucepans. In fact, since you're lugging everything around in a backpack, you'll probably only have one.

So you've got to think in terms of simple dishes. Very simple.

The secret of cooking over a fire is to use its natural characteristics. It can be far more versatile than you might imagine.

For example, potatoes can be wrapped in foil and baked in the ashes at the margin of the fire while the filling cooks in the saucepan hanging over it. Meanwhile, you could be using long skewers to grill wild mushrooms or to toast some bread, to be eaten with a dip.

The type of food brought with you depends very much on the number of days away from shops. If it's a question of one night you can probably manage heavy and bulky things like potatoes and even, say, a tin of baked beans as a filling. For longer treks away from civilisation you're going to have to rely on dehydrated products.

TIPS ❧

○ Various things can be threaded on to wooden skewers and arranged over the fire or held there while you discuss the day's events – don't worry, the skewers won't catch fire before your food does. Skewer food includes bread, mushrooms, sausages, tofu, tomatoes, onions and garlic.

○ Rather than trying to make a sauce, bring along tomato paste (and dilute it with water) plus some tangy dips in leak-proof plastic containers.

○ Food can taste rather bland out of doors so pop some curry powder and a selection of herbs into your backpack.

○ Take a little flour with you. It has all kinds of uses.

Rule of thumb ━○

Getting enough food when you're hiking in the wilderness can be a problem. You may need half as many calories again as when at home or work:

○ Maintenance at a desk job – 15 calories per pound (33 calories per kilo) of body weight per day.
○ Hiking – 20 calories per pound (44 calories per kilo) of body weight per day.
○ Strenuous hiking – 25 calories per pound (55 calories per kilo) of body weight per day.

WILD MUSHROOMS 🍄

Generally speaking, in order to preserve the flavour, you shouldn't wash the wild mushrooms you've collected (see previous chapter). Just give them a wipe. But make an exception for the morel whose deep pits may hide insects and grit. Discard the spongy part from ceps and similar species which have pores.

Cooking mushrooms without pans

Thread whole or sliced mushrooms on to wooden skewers, according to size. Parasol and Shaggy Parasol mushrooms are so large you'll only get one per skewer. Brush with oil (and herbs, if you have them). Then arrange yourself by the fire, take hold of a skewer, and watch your mushrooms cook.

The morel, being hollow, can be stuffed, then wrapped in foil and cooked in the ashes.

Cooking mushrooms with pans

Most mushrooms are excellent fried in a little olive oil with garlic and parsley but some benefit from a little extra care:

❂ **Cep**. Slice and gently fry. Then add tomato purée, water (or wine) and herbs. Use as a pasta sauce.

❂ **Chanterelle**. Very nice in omelettes or with scrambled eggs or as a sort of stew with onions, white wine, lemon juice and parsley.

❂ **Morel**. Blanch before cooking. Like the chanterelle, very good in omelettes or with scrambled eggs and in soups and stews.

❂ **Oyster mushroom**. The rather rubbery flesh needs careful cooking. Roll in flour and fry.

❂ **Wood Hedgehog**. Boil to remove the bitter taste. Discard the water and boil in milk or stock for about 20 minutes. Serve on bread toasted on skewers.

○ **Parasol and Shaggy Parasol**. Properly cooked, the flesh can resemble veal. Remove the stems and fry in olive oil on both sides with garlic and parsley. Serve with lemon wedges.

DANDELIONS

While eating the leaves as a salad you can roast the roots in foil in the camp fire. For a pan they should be chopped, sautéed and finally stewed to make them soft.

NETTLES

Nettles also make rather good soup. Take a few handfuls of the *young* leaves, wash them and heat them in a closed pan without adding any more water until everything has wilted down. Strain off any liquid, add a generous knob of butter plus seasoning and continue simmering for a further five minutes, mashing now and then. Tip the purée out onto a plate. Prepare a thick stock using butter, flour, a stock cube and water. When the stock is ready add back the purée and stir.

FENNEL

Take the fennel roots, wrap in foil and bake in the ashes of the fire. Fennel tends to take up the flavour of other things it's cooked with so you could add strips of, say, orange peel before wrapping in the foil.

SWEET CHESTNUTS

Sweet chestnuts can be boiled but they're best roasted on the camp fire. Slit them all first – except one – and put them in the hot ashes; when the unslit chestnut explodes the others should be ready.

WOOD SORREL 🐌

The best way of dealing with wood sorrel is to make it into soup.

1 onion
1 carrot
2 tbsp flour
Butter or olive oil
4 handfuls of wood sorrel
2 pints of stock (prepared by adding a stock cube to hot water)

Chop the onion and the carrot and sauté in butter or oil. Add the flour and sauté for two minutes. Add the sorrel and, when wilted, add the stock. Simmer for about four minutes.

MARSH SAMPHIRE/GLASSWORT 🐌

Wash the whole plant well and boil it upside down with the roots. Then serve with melted butter or some other dressing. Slide each stem between your teeth to remove the more succulent flesh from the tougher spine (rather as with artichoke leaves).

CARRAGHEEN OR IRISH MOSS 🐌

Add one mug of seaweed to three mugs of water and simmer slowly until the weed has dissolved. Once cool you'll have jelly. Or if you simmer it in milk you'll have blancmange. Add flavouring, if you have something.

LAVERBREAD 🐌

Laverbread isn't really bread but it is very tasty. Wash the laver and, like spinach, simmer it in a little water until you have a purée. Let it cool. Shape in accordance with your artistic inclinations, coat with flour and fry.

COOKING 'REAL' BREAD

Put some flour in a container (4oz/100g will make about six flat breads) and slowly add water. Mix in with your fingers and knead for at least five minutes. Form into a ball, cover with a damp cloth and set aside for half an hour. When ready, take a lump of dough and flatten it as best you can between your hands. Dust it with flour and slap it into a hot lightly-oiled pan (it may be easier if you turn your pan upside-down and cook on the bottom of it like a griddle). Cook for about a minute, then turn it over and finish it off for half a minute on the other side. As an extra refinement, brown it here and there in the flames of the fire (or stove).

COLD WEATHER TIPS

- If you're using a stove on snow put some insulation down first, such as a piece of wood. Otherwise your stove will melt the snow and possibly topple over. Or dig down to firm ground.
- If you're using a gas canister you may need to warm it up. Try putting it inside your clothing.

LEAVE NO TRACE

When you've finished with the campsite tidy everything up so there's no trace of your fire or your cooking.

- Bury the ashes or sprinkle them unobtrusively.

- Replace turf, if you were forced to dig it up and set it aside.

- Replace any hearth stones where they came from.

- Don't wash plates and pans in a stream. Instead collect some water and move off 20 paces or so. Only use non-detergent, biodegradable soap.

CAMPING IN THE WILD

Camping out can be a privilege or it can be purgatory. It all depends on how you go about it – and on the weather.

✸ WHERE TO CAMP ✸

The ideal wild camping spot has the following characteristics:

LOW IMPACT 🔖

○ Camp preferably on land where there's no vegetation to be spoiled – on forest duff or on bare sand or earth.

○ Camp at lower elevations – high up, especially above the tree line, plants have a hard enough time without having to contend with tents being put on top of them.

○ Don't camp too near to water – you may frighten away the animals that depend on it.

○ Avoid ecotones – they're the key places for wildlife where two ecosystems meet, such as where a forest joins grassland.

○ Don't start 'engineering works' by moving stones and logs and uprooting bushes; if the site isn't suitable, find another one.

Rule of thumb —○

Move frequently – don't stay at the same site for more than three nights.

COMFORT

○ The ground needs to be flat. Lie down on it to test it. It's permissible to remove stones and bits of wood. If the ground isn't perfectly flat pitch the tent with your head uphill.

○ Remember that cold air sinks and that river bottoms, gorges and basins can be much colder in the night and early morning than land a little higher up.

○ For a quick getaway in the morning, pitch your tent where it will catch the early sunshine – for example, on the east-facing side of a hill. That way, everything has a better chance of drying before you pack up.

○ In wind try to find a sheltered spot and pitch your tent with the door facing away from it.

SAFETY

○ Don't pitch your tent where it's likely to be inundated in heavy rain or where stones and boulders dislodged from above might crash down on it.

○ To stop the spread of fire there should be six good paces between tents.

TIPS ❧

○ If you're trying to anchor a tent from which a guy line has become torn off, or if you're trying to anchor a tarpaulin which has no attachment points, place a pebble under the fabric where you want to attach your line and then make a noose around the fabric and the pebble. That way, the fabric can't slide through the knot.
○ If the ground is too hard for tent pegs, find some suitable rocks and tie the guy ropes to those.

WILD CAMPING AND THE LAW 🐾

In England and Wales there is no general right to camp wild. You may be trespassing. Therefore, whenever practicable you should:

○ Ask permission from the landowner.

However, there is a convention that in the more remote mountain areas wild camping will be tolerated.

In Scotland the position is different. The Land Reform (Scotland) Act 2003 and Scottish Outdoor Access Code, which came into force in 2005, established a statutory right to camp. You can see the Code at: **www.outdooraccess-scotland.com**

❋ KEEPING WARM AT NIGHT ❋

Hopefully you've come well prepared for the conditions but if you're feeling cold in your sleeping bag:

○ Get up and run around a bit. When you return to your sleeping bag you'll warm it up very quickly.

◎ Wear a hat.

◎ Put plastic bags over your hands and feet to act as 'vapour barriers' and then put gloves and socks on top.

◎ Increase the amount of insulation by arranging things under and over the bag – your backpack and outer clothing, for example.

◎ Try to make sure your bag is perfectly dry for the following night by airing it in the sun.

IS IT BETTER TO DRESS OR UNDRESS? 🐾

A sleeping bag acts rather like a thermos flask. If you put something cold in it, it stays cold. If you put something warm in it, it stays warm. You can maximise the warming effect by taking some brisk exercise and then getting into the bag naked, or nearly so. The heat you give off will then make the bag toasty warm. It's better to put any available extra insulation around the bag rather than around you. If you're seriously cold, share a sleeping bag with someone else.

WHEN TO UNPACK YOUR SLEEPING BAG 🐾

Sleeping bags that have been crammed into stuff sacks need a while to recover their loft, which is what gives them their insulating properties. On the other hand, you don't want them getting damp:

◎ When the air is dry, unpack your bag as early as possible to let it expand.

◎ When the air is humid leave your bag packed until you're ready to get into it.

If you're using a down bag or one of the synthetics that's damaged by washing, use something to keep your sweat and body oil off the bag – a sleeping bag liner or clothes.

Rule of thumb —O
If you're sleeping outside without a tent then put your sleeping bag under a tree. It will reduce the heat loss and stop the dew making your bag so wet in the morning.

❊ TOILET AND WASTE ❊ ARRANGEMENTS

If there are only a few of you, you can make your own individual arrangements.

THE INDIVIDUAL CAT HOLE

Use a trowel to excavate a hole about 4in (10cm) deep, at least 50 paces from water, the path and the camp. Unless there is the danger of starting a fire, paper should be burned in the hole – paper can take a long time to decompose. Fill the hole back in, replacing the grass if there was grass, and leave the area at least as good as it was before.

Only if it's impossible to dig a hole should you try to find a rock you can roll aside. Use the depression and then replace the rock.

TAMPONS AND SANITARY TOWELS

Do not try to bury these. Put them in a container (together with a tea bag to absorb odours) and pack them out with you.

LITTER 🐚

○ Collect all litter, including other people's, and pack it out with you.

○ Do *not* put cans and other litter under stones or inside stone cairns.

✹ TAKING CHILDREN ✹

Some youngsters love the outdoors (and will hopefully find the information in this book very useful). But others hate it or just aren't old enough to appreciate it. If yours are in the latter category then you're going to need a little ingenuity.

BABIES 🐚

Very young children are the easiest because they can always be put in a baby-carrier.

○ A baby can't go in a backpack-style baby carrier until she or he can sit upright (at least six months).

Remember:

○ The baby will need to be dressed more warmly than you are.

○ A favourite toy should be tied to the baby carrier.

○ Don't go walking under any low branches when using a back-pack-style carrier.

INFANTS 🐚

From the age of around two an infant is too heavy to go in a baby-carrier but too small to walk very far. Hiking trips are out until the age of about five but that doesn't stop you going on picnics.

From five onwards you can start hiking together as a family again. But don't expect to go very far. Start off with, maybe, a mile. Keep it fun. Don't let a child ever associate hiking with discomfort, suffering, cold, damp, boredom or misery. One slip and you can spoil family hiking for years to come.

OLDER CHILDREN

Give them some responsibility and involve them in the decisions. For example, give them duties suitable for their ages and abilities such as:

- Carrying their own equipment in a backpack
- Collecting firewood and making tinder and kindling
- Finding and collecting water
- Map reading and route finding

SAFETY

As a general rule, for both adults and children, if you start out together you should stick together. But most kids go through a period when they hate to be seen with their parents. And hiking becomes much more exciting if they think they're actually leading the 'expedition'.

So there needs to be room for a little flexibility. Go through the maps with them and let them walk on ahead a little bit and 'scout out' the route. If you do allow this there are some rules that will avoid problems.

- Don't let them go on ahead if you know there's a fork coming up in the path.

◉ Establish a 'contact procedure' which requires them to sit and wait for you every five minutes or so.

◉ Arm them with some communication device. It could be a mobile phone, it could be a walkie-talkie or it could be a whistle (but make sure they know not to blow it except in emergency).

ENTERTAINMENT 🎧

Of course, there's nothing to stop you taking portable electronic games along on a hike but it's nice if you can create some entertainment from the outdoors itself. That way kids have something extra to enjoy that they can't get at home.

Route-finding games

Young children can fairly easily be taken in with tales of smugglers' paths, secret treasure and the like. Prepare a few notes before setting off and 'age' them by burning the edges or warming them in the oven or rubbing them in some dirt. The first note might say something like:

◉ *Go to the three pine trees. Captain Jack.*

When the kids aren't looking you put the note somewhere they're sure to spot it.

Then the hunt is on. You don't have to know what's coming up ahead. Just make sure you have a good supply of notes for various different situations (*Proceed to the lookout . . . You'll find what you're seeking by the big rock . . .* and so on.) All you have to do is hide an appropriate note at the appropriate place while the kids are busy hunting around. And then . . . hey presto . . . Wow, it's the next clue!

For older children things could be a little more sophisticated. For example, you could hide some 'treasure' and send the kids off to find it by:

○ Marking the location on the map
○ Giving compass bearings
○ Giving the location by GPS (Global Positioning System)

Tracking games

As a variation on route-finding games, the traditional 'hide and seek' can become a sort of tracking game in the larger expanse of the great outdoors. Somebody goes off and makes a trail – a deliberate footprint here, a broken branch there, a fragment of material and so on – and the others try to follow after a suitable interval.

Some other ideas

○ From the chapter on *Tracks*, collect bird pellets and tease them apart to see what they contain; see who can be the first to spot and identify a track.

○ From the chapter on *Coastline*, have with you an underwater viewing tube and use it to watch and identify the life in ponds and rock pools.

○ From the chapter on *Knots*, see who can be the first to tie a particular type; set up a rope and see if anyone can manage to attach a Prusik loop (see pages 122–124).

○ From the chapter on the *Night sky*, see who can identify the most stars or who can find north.

○ From the chapter on *Wild food* see who can collect the most edible plants for dinner.

○ From the chapter on the *Weather*, see who can name the clouds.

Route finding

Scientists have yet to find any direction-finding mechanism in the human brain. And yet it does seem that some people do have a 'good sense of direction' while others don't. What's the secret? In fact, there isn't any magic to it. It's just a question of establishing a simple map in your brain and then relating what you see on the ground to this template.

❋ MAPS ❋

Hopefully, before setting off, you had a good look at a map and packed it in your rucksack.

For hiking purposes you need a scale of either:

- ⊙ 1:25,000 which means 1cm on the map represents 250m on the ground

- ⊙ 1:50,000 which means 1cm on the map represents 500m on the ground.

HOW FAR IS IT? 🥾

In reality, distances can often be somewhat further than apparent from the map.

Flat maps cannot take into account the extra distance walked as the ground climbs and falls. If you know your Pythagoras' theorem you'll recognise that if you cover a distance of three miles, as shown on the map, but also ascend to a height of one mile (5,280 feet) then the actual distance covered will be an extra 282 yards.

What's more, wiggly paths are the norm in hilly or mountainous areas but the map just can't show every little meander. So take a piece of cotton, lay it out along the path marked on the map and then measure it off along the scale printed on the map.

Rule of thumb ─○

In hilly or mountainous terrain add about 10% to apparent distances to allow for the effects described above.

WHAT'S THE TERRAIN LIKE?

The contour lines on the map can give you a lot of information:

○ If the contour lines are close together the terrain is steep.

○ If the contour lines are far apart the terrain is gentle.

○ If the path follows a contour line it's neither ascending nor descending.

○ If the path cuts across the contour lines it's either ascending or descending.

The heights of the main (thicker) contour lines are marked on them somewhere but it isn't always easy to find the numbers. So how do you know if your route is going up or going down? Usually there will be other clues on the map. For example, if you're not sure if you're looking at a ridge or a valley bottom on the map then:

○ If there's a stream marked, it must be a valley bottom because streams don't run along ridges.

HOW LONG WILL IT TAKE? 🍃

It's a good general rule that a hike always takes longer than you think it will. Once you become experienced you'll know your own pace. In the meantime work on the basis of:

○ 4 km/h (2.5m/h) on flat ground plus one hour for every 300m (1000 feet) of ascent.

Rule of thumb —○

Times given on hiking signs or in guide books don't normally allow for any stops. Increase them by about a third to allow for rests and taking in the view.

✻ NAVIGATING ✻

NAVIGATING BY THE SUN 🍃

In the northern hemisphere:

○ The sun rises in the east.
○ The sun is at its highest in the south around midday.
○ The sun sets in the west.

These directions are only approximate. For example, where the sun comes into view in the morning isn't *precisely* east, merely in a roughly easterly direction:

○ At the equinoxes (mid-March and mid-September) sunrise and sunset are very close to due east and due west.

○ In mid-summer (mid-June) the sun rises in the north-east and sets in the north-west.

○ In mid-December the sun rises in the south-east and sets in the south-west.

The Stick Trick (version 1)

Step 1. Plant a straight stick into flat, even ground at an angle towards the sun so that no shadow is produced.

Step 2. Wait until a shadow appears; it will run roughly east – west.

The stick trick works at any time of day and doesn't require a very long wait.

The Stick Trick (version 2)

Step 1. Plant a straight stick vertically into flat, even ground.

Step 2. Place a small stone at the end of the shadow.

Step 3. Wait about 15 minutes for the shadow to move and place a second stone at the end of this shadow.

Step 4. Draw a line between the two stones; it will run roughly east – west.

The Watch Trick

Step 1. Holding the watch horizontally and level, point the hour hand towards the spot on the ground that appears to be directly under the sun.

Step 2. North will be halfway between the hour hand and 12 o'clock. Note that before noon you'll have to go round the watch face *anticlockwise* to find the mid-point; after noon you'll have to go round the watch face *clockwise* to find the mid-point.

○ Example: At 9am north will be at 4.30 on the dial.

This is only a very approximate method but it helps. You can improve it if you set your watch to local sun time. How? The method given below also allows you to know when it's noon without having a watch.

Telling the time by the sun

Step 1. Begin by setting up the Stick Trick version 2 in the late morning.

Step 2. Extend the east-west line so you can draw a second line from the base of the stick to join the east-west line at right angles.

Step 3. When the shadow of the stick falls along the new line it is local noon by the sun.

Navigating when the sky is covered

If the sky is covered, vegetation can provide a *rough* clue. Many trees, especially conifers, are more bushy on their south-facing sides. By contrast, moss grows most abundantly on the north side of trees. Knowledge of the terrain will help. For example, if there's a stream or river do you know where it's headed?

You may be able to make your own compass using a needle (or similar). You'll also need to find a magnet, but you'd be surprised how many things have one. There's always a magnet in the speaker of any radio, for example. Stroke the needle in one direction only, always using the same side of the magnet. Once the needle is magnetised either suspend it or float it in a cup of water on a sliver of cork. It will orientate itself north-south and, with a bit of luck, you'll be able to work out which is which.

NAVIGATING BY THE STARS

Method 1

You can always work out the points of the compass if you can identify Polaris/the Pole Star, which appears to remain in a fixed place more or less at true north. To locate it, first find the distinctive pattern of stars known as the Big Dipper. The two stars that form the end of the Dipper's 'pot' point straight at Polaris. For full details see the chapter about the *Night sky*.

Method 2

If Polaris is obscured but you can still see some stars, then:

○ Where the stars are rising is approximately east

○ Where the stars are setting is approximately west

○ If a star you are watching is moving to the right you are facing approximately south

○ If a star you are watching is moving to the left you are facing approximately north

To make it easier to see which way a star is moving bang two sticks vertically into the ground a pace or so apart so that, like the sights of a rifle, they point directly at your chosen star.

NAVIGATING BY THE MOON

Method 1

○ Where the full moon rises is east
○ Where the full moon is at midnight is south
○ Where the full moon sets is west

Method 2

If there's a quarter moon, draw in your mind's eye a line from the upper tip to the lower tip and continue it on down to the horizon. Where the line touches the horizon is approximately south.

NAVIGATING WITH A COMPASS 🧭

When using a compass, keep it away from sources of magnetism. You won't get an accurate reading inside a car, for example, nor if the compass is held close to a pair of binoculars or a camera.

True north, magnetic north and grid north

Fortunately we happen to live on a planet on which a freely rotating magnetised needle always points more or less to north. But:

⊙ Magnetic north as indicated by a compass changes over the years and is normally slightly different from true north.

⊙ Grid north, as indicated by the grid lines on a map, may also be slightly different from both magnetic north and true north.

However, for the purposes of compass navigation in Britain the differences between the 'three norths' are generally not sufficient to cause a significant problem and can usually be ignored.

How to use a compass

A basic compass is just a magnetised needle inside a round container. Hopefully, your compass is a little more sophisticated with the following features:

⊙ A straight-edged transparent base-plate with a direction arrow on it.

❂ A compass housing with a rotating bezel mounted on the base
plate.

This kind of compass is designed not just to determine where
north is but also to help you walk a compass bearing between two
points – the place you now are and the place you would like to be.
If you don't use this sort of compass regularly it's easy to become
confused. Here are the key things to remember.

Walking a compass course

Step 1. Unfold the map and lay it out on a convenient flat surface.

Step 2. Make sure that north as indicated on the rotating bezel of
the compass is lined up with its mark and then place the compass
on the map so that the direction arrow on the base plate as well as
north on the compass bezel both point precisely to the top of the
map.

Step 3. Gently turn the map, with the compass on it, until north as
indicated by the compass needle is lined up with the north marker
on the bezel.

❂ *You now have the map and the compass orientated with the
real world.*

Step 4. Read off the compass course (bearing) you would need to
follow between your first point and your second point. (Obviously
you can move the compass across the map but always keep the
base plate aligned, as before, with the grid lines.)

Step 5. Rotate the bezel on the compass until the bearing you just
worked out is lined up with the direction arrow on the base plate.

Step 6. Hold the compass in front of your chest so the direction
arrow is pointing away from you.

Step 7. This is the tricky part. Still holding the compass as described, *rotate yourself* (*not* the compass) until the red end of the needle lines up with the north position on the bezel. You should now be facing the way you want to go.

Step 8. Look along the compass bearing and note any landmarks such as a church, lake or summit.

Step 9. Check that the landmarks correspond with the map. If so you can proceed to the next step.

Step 10. Fold up the map and set off towards the landmark. (In the absence of any landmark or in mist you'll have to keep the compass out and follow the direction arrow on the base plate, with the compass held as in Step 7.)

Finding your position

Step 1. Identify a landmark.

Step 2. Point the direction arrow on your base plate at it.

Step 3. Keeping the direction arrow pointed at the landmark, rotate the bezel until north on the bezel coincides with north as indicated by the compass needle.

Step 4. Find the landmark on the map.

Step 5. Without disturbing the bezel, place the compass on the map so that a long edge is touching the landmark and *the grid lines printed on the compass base are parallel with the grid lines on the map.*

Step 6. Using a pencil, draw a line on the map along the compass edge from the landmark and going in the direction that you are from the landmark.

Step 7. Repeat the procedure with one or two more landmarks. Where the lines intersect is where you are.

Sometimes it isn't possible to identify more than one landmark but that can sometimes be enough. Draw your one line as described above. *You are somewhere on that line.* Search along it for a clue to your exact position. Maybe there's a stream, a path, an outcrop or a dip that will pin things down more precisely.

✳ LOST ✳

Some people will never admit to being lost while others tend to panic very easily. If you think you're lost while out hiking the first thing to do is:

⊙ Stop, calm down and think.

Don't go rushing about making the situation worse. It's very unlikely that you're as lost as you imagine you are. For example, if you set off from Fort William an hour ago you know you're a couple of miles or so from Fort William. That's already pretty good. And presumably you know which way you were headed when you set off. Was it, for example, towards the rising sun, the east? Then Fort William must lie a couple of miles or so to the west.

Rules of thumb ━○
⊙ Don't follow a mountain stream down on the grounds it must come out somewhere. Streams tend to follow the shortest route – in other words the steepest and most dangerous.
⊙ Don't split up.
⊙ Don't dump your backpack while searching around – you may not be able to find it later and it may contain things you need.

- If you can easily hike up to a good lookout point then do so but make sure you can find your way back to where you are now.
- If you've lost the path then walk a *search pattern*. That is to say, methodically trace an ever-growing spiral out from your present position. At some point you must intersect with the path.

TIP ✿

When you're a little unsure of your exact position there's a technique called *missing on purpose* that can help. For example, suppose you're headed across open ground towards the road along which you've parked your car. Because you're slightly lost you won't know, once you hit the road, whether your car will be to your right or to your left. This is where *missing on purpose* is useful. You take a direction which means you'll miss your car either well to the left or well to the right. Let's say you've gone to the right. Then when you hit the path you know the car must be to the left.

DANGERS AND FIRST AID

It's probably more dangerous to stay inside than to be outdoors. Nevertheless, keeping safe in the British countryside does call for a little knowledge.

❋ LIGHTNING ❋

You stand more chance of winning the Lottery than of being struck by lightning. Even so, it's not a great idea to be standing on top of a wind-blasted, rain-soaked mountain as lightning approaches. If your hair stands on end it's not because you got the hair gel mixed up with the glue. It means an imminent lightning strike is probable at that spot.

● Get down to somewhere safe.

● If you're caught out, get rid of *everything* metal. A strike close by will cause metal to heat up and burn you (now you see why your mother told you not to have that piercing).

● Get some insulation between you and the ground (sleeping mat, rubber-soled boots etc.).

● Crouch down with your feet together, your hands on your knees and your head tucked in.

Safe places

❍ Indoors, away from metal pipes and electrical wiring

❍ In a car or metal shelter

❍ Inside a deep cave

❍ On the valley floor

❍ Among the lowest trees in a forest

❍ Among the lowest boulders where there are other higher boulders

Dangerous places

❍ High ground

❍ Under an isolated tree

❍ At the foot of cliffs

❍ Close to large metal objects

❍ Any place you are the highest object

❋ COLD ❋

You've got all your clothing on and yet you're still cold. In fact, there may be a few things you've overlooked:

❍ Put plastic bags on your feet and then your socks and shoes/boots on top.

❍ Put plastic bags on your hands and then your gloves on top.

❍ In a real emergency, try wearing a dustbin bag over your torso with your clothes on top.

The idea is to create a 'vapour barrier' that will reduce heat loss due to evaporation.

HYPOTHERMIA

On cold days, watch for signs of hypothermia in yourself and others. The most dangerous time is when air temperatures are from around 50°F (10°C) down to just below freezing. At lower temperatures people tend to treat the conditions more seriously and, what's more, it can't rain. Wet clothing is the enemy so:

○ Avoid sweating – don't wear more clothing than you need when active.

○ Avoid getting your clothes wet with rain.

Normal body temperature is 98.6°F (37°C). It shouldn't go much lower:

○ Less than 95°F (35°C) – hypothermia begins with shivering, slurred speech and clumsy actions.

○ 84°F–90°F (29°C–32°C) – victim is drowsy, confused and unable to answer simple questions.

○ 77°F–84°F (25°C–29°C) – victim unconscious.

○ Below 77°F (25°C) – victim *appears* dead but may not be.

Treatment of hypothermia

The professionals have special equipment for treating hypothermia. While waiting for them:

○ Get the victim to shelter and remove wet clothes.

- Put the person naked into a sleeping bag with another naked person for effective skin-to-skin heat exchange.

- If the victim is able to drink, provide something at around body temperature *not* hot.

- Do *not* give alcohol.

In severe cases:

- Be extremely careful carrying a victim as physical shocks could cause death.

- Apply hot towels or similar to the head, neck, sides of the chest and groin.

- Breathe warm air into the victim's mouth to assist heating of the body core.

- Do *not* heat the hands or feet – if you do, blood will rush to those parts causing cold blood to move to the core and chill it even further.

❋ HEAT ❋

Overheating comes in two stages, *heat exhaustion* and *heat stroke*. You're most likely to suffer in humid conditions when sweat can't evaporate to cool you down.

HEAT EXHAUSTION

Symptoms: Your skin is cold and sweaty and you feel sick and faint.

Avoidance: Don't walk too fast in hot weather or wearing too many clothes. Rest during the hottest part of the day. Drink more than you think you need. Wear a hat.

Treatment: Sip water or, better still, a sports drink with electrolytes in it. Lie somewhere cool and shady with your head slightly down-hill.

HEAT STROKE

Symptoms: Your skin is dry, pink and warm. You feel unbearably hot. You become delirious.

Avoidance: As for heat exhaustion.

Treatment: Heat stroke is far more serious than heat exhaustion. It can be fatal. It means your body's cooling system has broken down. You can only be saved by *external* cooling – the application of wet cloths or even lying in water.

❋ BURNS ❋

Burns come in four major types:

◉ **First degree**. The least serious. Only the outer layer of skin (epidermis) is affected. The area will be red, swollen and painful. Treat with cool running water.

◉ **Second degree**. The epidermis and part of the next layer (dermis) are affected. The skin blisters. Again, cool running water will bring some relief. Apply a dry, sterile dressing only if the burn is large. The skin should recover in 10-14 days without scarring.

◉ **Third degree**. Destroys the entire thickness of the skin along with sweat glands, sebaceous glands, hair follicles, blood vessels and nerves – so there is no pain. The burnt area looks leathery. Urgent medical treatment is essential.

○ **Fourth degree**. The burn is deep, involving muscle and bone. The flesh looks charred. Extremely grave. Urgent medical treatment is essential.

It's worth remembering that any burned area, even when healed, will be extra sensitive to sun burn and should be kept out of the sun by using high factor sun cream for at least a year.

SUNBURN 🕯

Sunburn is no joke. In fact, it's essentially the same as any other burn. Even in Britain it can take under 30 minutes to do the damage and then it just goes on feeling worse, becoming most painful after 12-24 hours.

Avoidance: Limited exposure to sunlight is beneficial as it produces Vitamin D. Beyond that keep your skin covered and wear a hat. If it's too hot for long sleeves and trousers apply a sunscreen. The Sun Protection Factor (SPF) loosely indicates the amount of time you can be exposed without getting burnt relative to the amount of time without the sunscreen. In other words, if your skin would normally burn in 30 minutes an SPF of 20 should allow you to be in the sun for 10 hours. Certain drugs, including some antibiotics and acne medicines as well as St John's Wort, can make you more vulnerable.

Treatment: Treat mild sunburn with cold compresses of equal parts milk and water. Aloe-based products are also soothing. Severe sunburn can cause blistering, nausea, dehydration and the loss of electrolytes. So have plenty of sports drinks to replace them. Keep out of the sun until fully recovered.

✱ ANIMALS ✱

DOGS 🐾

Most dogs have barks far worse than their bites but there are always exceptions.

Avoidance: Dogs have a territory and some will defend it vigorously against intruders. If you can curve well away from the dog then do so. Never try to pat a strange dog. If a dog insists on coming after you don't use aggressive body language. Just keep walking steadily (but not further into its territory) in an unthreatening way. Don't run and, above all, don't let small children run – some dogs have an instinct to chase. If you're frightened of dogs you might like to carry a can with you. If a dog comes at you, pop a few pebbles into the can and shake it – the noise will make a lot of dogs back off.

Treatment: If someone gets bitten wash the wound as soon as possible. A deep wound should be flushed with clean water for around ten minutes to prevent infection. Fortunately, there is no rabies in Britain but tetanus shots should be given if they're not up to date.

FARM ANIMALS 🐾

Farm animals other than dogs (see above) aren't generally aggressive but they might approach in the hope of food. *Don't feed them.* It's bad for them and it's bad for other walkers. Normally, the only real dangers are:

◉ Getting between an animal and its young
◉ Getting between your dog and an animal that's charging it
◉ Getting in the way of a stampeding herd

○ Bulls on their own

In fact, it's quite rare for a bull to be running free in a field. In Britain they're usually kept in the love nest and are not, then, aggressive. If you're unsure of the sex:

○ A bull has a prominent tuft of hairs halfway along its belly.

If your footpath crosses a field of livestock, check to see if it's been closed (maybe a sign has blown down, for example). If the farmer hasn't seen fit to close it then it *should* be safe to proceed.

All that having been said, people are occasionally killed or injured by cows or other animals. Pay particular attention in windy weather which tends to make animals nervous.

Rule of thumb ─○

If you do get charged and you have a dog with you on a lead (as it should be) then unleash it. This will usually distract attention from you. Don't worry about Rover – he can always outmanoeuvre the enemy.

✿ FIRE ✿

In these days of hot dry summers even Britain is a fire risk zone. Here are the key ways to prevent fires:

○ Never throw cigarette ends down or out of car windows.

○ Never leave glass or bottles around as glass can magnify the sun's rays.

○ Never light a fire if there's the *slightest* risk of setting vegetation alight.

○ Pitch tents at least six good paces apart

○ Never light a stove inside a tent.

ACTION IN CASE OF FIRE 🐚

If the fire is *small* you may be able to:

○ Beat it out.
○ Pour water on it (if, say, you're near a stream).
○ Smother it by, for example, shovelling earth over it.
○ Create a fire break downwind.

If not:

○ Evacuate the area.
○ Dial 999 as soon as you can.
○ Give the location as accurately as possible.

✹ INSECTS ✹

In the UK, insects are generally more annoying than dangerous – unless you have an allergy.

FLYING INSECTS 🐚

Rules of thumb ⊶

○ To avoid nasty bites and stings apply an insect repellent. Eating one or two cloves of raw garlic a day seems to help. Keep away from the nests of bees, wasps and hornets.
○ Try not to scratch itchy bites – they'll clear up much more quickly if you leave them alone. Try to remove a bee stinger if it has remained in the skin, but be careful not to squeeze any more poison into the body.

○ Bee stings can be neutralised in a weak solution of bicarbonate of soda.
○ Vinegar or lemon will counter the pain of wasp or hornet stings; vinegar is also good on hairy caterpillar rashes.
○ Ant bites respond well to eau de Cologne.

Most instances of serious or fatal allergic reactions to stings occur within the first hour.

○ You can always expect localised pain, redness and swelling at the site of, say, a wasp sting.
○ If the reaction is more extensive, antihistamine tablets and creams will help.
○ If there are breathing difficulties, swelling of the mouth or throat, nausea, chest pain and faintness then urgent treatment is called for.

Anyone who knows they are seriously allergic should carry the appropriate medical kit with them.

TICKS 🐛

Ticks look like lentils with little legs. They drop on to you from long grass, bushes and trees. Their bites are not painful but they can transmit Lyme disease which has a whole range of debilitating symptoms.

Avoidance

Wear light-coloured clothing in tick country – the New Forest and other similar areas in the south of England are hot spots. You'll then be able to spot the ticks. If you feel anything crawling on your skin investigate at once. At the end of each day strip off and examine yourself for ticks.

Treatment

If you find a tick attached to your skin get it off immediately. The longer it's attached the greater the risk of transmission of Lyme disease – it seems to take a few hours. Touching it with, say, the head of a match immediately after it's blown out may make it back off. Or a spot of fuel from the camping stove will make it relax its grip. If you have a pair of tweezers take hold of it by its tiny head and pull – don't squeeze the body or you may discharge its stomach contents into your bloodstream. If you don't have tweezers, improvise. Keep the tick in a container and see a doctor as soon as possible.

❋ SNAKES ❋

The adder (*Vipera berus*) is the only indigenous poisonous snake in the UK. It can be identified by a sort of blackish indented zig-zag marking all along the back, against a background colour that varies from grey to brown and even reddish.

NON-VENOMOUS SNAKES THAT MIGHT BE CONFUSED WITH AN ADDER

- Grass snake. Similar colour but the markings are mostly on the sides and take the form of dark dots or short splodgy oblongs which are not connected together. Grass snakes also have a thin yellow band on the neck, which adders do not.

- Smooth snake. You'll be lucky to see this in Britain. Again, similar in colour to the adder but the marks along the back are in two lines of small, dark splodges.

- Slow-worm. This is actually a legless lizard, not a snake. It has a small head and a very shiny body. Mature male slow worms often have blue spots – mature females and young have a black line down the centre of their backs.

Avoidance

Adders are widespread in Britain but are most usually seen on heaths in the south of England in spring and autumn when they're rather sluggish (they hibernate in winter). Just watch where you're walking (and sitting) and wear stout footwear and trousers in long grass – it can be a good idea to swish the grass ahead of you with a stick. If you see a snake don't try to pick it up.

Treatment

If you're bitten by an adder the first rule is *don't panic.* The fact that you've been bitten does *not* mean that venom has been injected. Even if it has the effects are seldom very serious. No one has died from an adder bite in the UK for 30 years. The correct procedure is:

- Keep calm.
- If the bite was on an arm, immobilise it with a splint.
- If the bite was on a leg, immobilise it as soon as practicable (you may need your leg to walk for help).
- Go to hospital.

Do *not* try to suck out the venom or apply a tourniquet or a bandage.

POISONOUS PLANTS

The commonest problem plant in Britain is the stinging nettle.

If you brush against one just ignore the itching and it will go away in a few minutes.

But quite a lot of plants are dangerous if eaten. Never eat anything you're not 100 per cent sure of. Best-known no-nos include:

- Deadly nightshade
- Mistletoe
- Buttercup
- Rhubarb leaves
- Rhododendron
- Yew
- Oleander
- Potato flowers
- Foxglove
- Laburnum
- Privet
- Virginia creeper

❋ QUICKSAND AND BOGS ❋

Very *Famous Five* this one, but not as dangerous as some films would have you think. The main risk zones for quicksand in the UK are Morecambe Bay, the Dorset coast, the River Nith estuary close to the Solway Firth in Scotland and the River Dee estuary in Wales. Quicksand is a mixture of fine sand, clay and water and can appear solid when, in reality, it's sloppy and sticky. If you step into it don't panic and, above all, don't flail around:

- If you're wearing a backpack take it off.
- Tip yourself backwards as if swimming backstroke.
- Gradually ease your feet up to the surface.
- Slowly inch your way to terra firma.

The same techniques apply if you get stuck in a bog. Main boggy areas in the UK are Foxtor Mire and Raybarrow Pool on Dartmoor, Bleaklow Plateau in the Peak District, Northumberland National Park (especially the Cheviots), north-west Sutherland, Lewis and Orkney.

❋ ROCKFALLS ❋

Avalanches aren't very common in Britain but rockfalls are something you need to take a little more seriously. When your path takes you under a cliff:

○ Watch out for areas where there are piles of rocks or boulders – they may have fallen from above.

○ Listen for people above you – they might inadvertently dislodge stones.

○ Spread out – you don't all need to get hit.

○ Be especially careful after ice or rain as this will encourage loose pieces to fall.

○ When climbing always wear a helmet.

❋ CUT OFF BY THE TIDE ❋

See page 101 in the *Coastline* section.

❋ FIRST AID ❋

What should you do if somebody is injured or taken ill and can't get back to civilisation? Should you stay with the injured person or should you go for help?

This is a tricky question to which there can never be a definitive answer. Ideally you should have a mobile phone (and coverage) and there should be at least three of you (allowing one to stay and one to go for help).

But for the purposes of this exercise we'll assume there are two of you and no mobile phone. There's basically a three-step procedure:

○ Save life
○ Stabilise the situation
○ Get the victim out

SAVING LIFE AND STABILISING THE SITUATION

Sprains

Sprains are tears or general damage to the tough elastic ligaments attached to bones and holding joints in place. Most often sprains will occur in ankles, knees or the arches of the feet.

Rule of thumb ―○

As a general rule, the more the pain the more severe the sprain.

For first aid remember the acronym PRICE:

○ **P**rotect the injured limb
○ **R**est the injured limb
○ **I**ce the area
○ **C**ompress the area
○ **E**levate the limb

Fractures

There may be a lot of pain and possibly swelling. If the fracture is to a leg, immobilise it with a splint; for an arm either splint it or strap it to the body.

Choking

You'll choke when something gets lodged in the throat or windpipe cutting off the flow of air. It's usually food although with young children it can be anything. If the problem seems severe (the casualty can't respond or lips seem to be turning blue) you'll have to perform the *Heimlich Manoeuvre*:

- Stand behind the person.

- Wrap your arms around the waist.

- Tip the person forward slightly.

- Make a fist with one hand.

- Position it slightly above the navel of the casualty.

- Grasp the fist with your other hand.

- Press hard into the abdomen of the casualty as if trying to lift them.

- Repeat until the blockage is dislodged.

You can perform this manoeuvre on yourself:

- Place a fist slightly above your navel.

- Grasp your fist with your other hand and bend over a hard surface (a log or a picnic table, for example).

- Shove your fist upward and inward.

Wounds

A wound that bleeds copiously can be very frightening so it's important to know that most bleeding can be stopped relatively easily:

○ If no dressing is available press with your fingers or your hand. For a large wound, try to pull the edges together.

○ If a dressing can be improvised place it over the wound and apply gentle pressure. If the blood soaks through add another dressing and, if necessary, another.

○ If it can be done without aggravating the problem, elevate an injured limb.

If the bleeding doesn't respond to these measures and bright red blood is coming out in spurts then an artery has been cut. You should be able to arrest the bleeding by pushing on a pressure point. Pressure points are places where arteries pass over bones close to the skin. Push with a thumb or finger for at least 10 minutes but *not more than 15 minutes* (otherwise tissues may be damaged). The main pressure points are:

○ The middle of the inside of the upper arm
○ Just below the crease on the inside of the elbow
○ In the crease between thigh and torso
○ The middle of the top of the thigh at the front
○ The neck, either side of the Adam's Apple

If a limb is involved and you can't find a suitable pressure point use a tourniquet just above the wound:

○ Don't use anything too thin or it might cut into the flesh – a handkerchief rolled up makes a suitable tourniquet.

- After knotting the tourniquet around the limb use a pencil or similar as a 'turnkey' to tighten it. When the bleeding stops tie the pencil into position.

- Completely release the tourniquet for one minute every 15 minutes or tissue damage will result.

- Remove the tourniquet once bleeding stops.

Tetanus

Deep wounds carry a risk of tetanus caused by the soil-dwelling *Clostridium tetani*. Tetanus can be fatal. Hopefully, you've been immunised already:

- First and second doses 4-8 weeks apart

- Third dose six months after the second

- Booster every ten years

If you haven't been immunised you should go to a doctor or hospital urgently after receiving a deep cut.

Head injury

- Keep the casualty still for a while with the head slightly higher than the body.

- Stop any bleeding with light pressure only in case of skull fracture.

- Observation is the most important action. Watch out for confusion, loss of balance, slurring of speech, vomiting or changes in breathing or alertness.

- Nose bleeds following a head injury should be considered potentially serious especially if the discharge is watery.

Artificial ventilation

If a person has stopped breathing for whatever reason you'll need to provide artificial ventilation (AV):

○ The casualty should be face up.

○ Tilt the head back slightly to open the airway.

○ Remove any foreign bodies from the mouth.

○ Pinch the casualty's nose shut and seal your own mouth around the victim's mouth.

○ Blow into the casualty's mouth while watching for the chest to rise.

○ Remove your mouth and watch for the casualty's chest to fall.

○ Continue in this way at a comfortable rate until the victim begins to breathe unaided.

When breathing resumes place the casualty in the **recovery position**:

○ Turn casualty onto the side.

○ Tilt chin forward in an open airway position and place one of the victim's hands under the side of the face.

○ Have one leg extended and the other bent.

Cardiopulmonary resuscitation

If a person's heart has stopped beating you'll need to perform cardiopulmonary resuscitation (CPR). This may have been due to a heart attack whose symptoms would have included:

- Tightness or pain in the chest
- Breathlessness
- Dizziness
- Pain spreading to shoulders, neck, jaw or arms
- Sweating
- Nausea

Or it may have been due to some other reason. *Do not perform CPR unless you are absolutely certain the heart has stopped beating* (no pulse and no audible heartbeat with your ear on the person's chest). A person whose heart is beating could actually be killed by CPR. *Never practise CPR on a person, only on a dummy.*

CPR is a combination of artificial ventilation (above) and chest compression (CC).

Step One: give 15 chest compressions

With the victim face up on a firm surface:

- Locate the bottom of the breastbone. Measure three fingers up and place the heel of your hand in that spot.

- Place your other hand on top.

- Keeping your arms straight, lean forward and depress the breastbone by around 2in (5cm).

- Lean back, leaving your hands in place.

- Repeat 15 times at a rate of about three compressions every two seconds.

For children the displacement of the breastbone should be less.

For infants only use finger pressure.

Step Two: give two rescue breaths

Breathing and blood circulation should obviously take place at the same time. If you are alone you will have to alternate between CC and AV:

○ After every 15 cycles of CC give two breaths of AV as described above.

If there are two rescuers, however, the tasks can be shared:

○ One of you performs five cycles of CC.
○ The other then performs one breath of AV.
○ And so on.

Do not stop until:

○ Help arrives

○ The casualty starts breathing (*but cease CC as soon as there's a pulse*)

○ You are too exhausted to continue

GETTING THE CASUALTY OUT 🦶

You've saved life and stabilised the situation. Now you have to decide how to get the victim out. There are three possibilities:

○ You assist the victim to slowly get out.

○ You leave on your own to get help.

○ You stay in the hope you can summon help by some means or that help will arrive by chance.

If, after first aid, the casualty can safely walk, albeit slowly and with assistance, and you're confident of getting back to civilisation before dark or bad weather, then that's probably the thing to do.

If the casualty can't move and there's little likelihood of summoning help or help arriving by chance then you must go for assistance:

○ Make the casualty as comfortable as possible. Hand over things you're unlikely to need yourself.

○ Do your best to locate the spot on your map. Take compass readings (see *Route finding*) or find the position by GPS.

○ Make sure rescuers will be able to find the injured person quickly and easily by marking the spot. Peg out some brightly-coloured spare clothing, for example, or stamp out the word 'HELP' in the snow or write it with pieces of timber.

○ Proceed to where you can most quickly get help but don't rush – your getting injured will only make the situation worse.

If you decide to stay then see *Survival Skills* page 80 for ways of attracting attention.

SURVIVAL SKILLS

In the wildest parts of Britain survival skills might some day come in handy.

�֍ WATER �֍

Don't try to eke out your water supply by, say, drinking a mouthful every hour. The most efficient way is:

❂ Wait as long as you can before drinking.

❂ When you can't ignore your thirst any longer, drink as much as you want (or have).

THE SOLAR STILL 🐾

Dig a hole about 3ft (1m) across and 1ft (30cm) deep. Put a container in the bottom. Place a plastic sheet over the hole and secure the edges with earth or stones. Finally, put a small weight in the middle of the plastic immediately over the container. The idea is that water evaporating from the ground will condense on the plastic sheet, run down the plastic until it reaches the point under the weight and then drip into the container.

TIPS ❀

❂ Leafy shrubs placed in the hole around the container will increase the yield.

○ If you have a suitable tube you can run it into the container so you can suck water out without disturbing the still.

Variation

You can enclose an entire plant with a plastic bag or the branch of a tree to collect the moisture given off. Make sure the bag is completely sealed. Arrange a collector so that the moisture running down the plastic walls will drip into it.

COLLECTING DEW

If you have a sponge or suitable cloth you can soak up the morning dew from smooth rocks and plants and squeeze it out into your water container.

Rule of thumb —○
Water from a solar still will always be fit to drink. Otherwise, in the absence of some type of purification, water can be strained through fabric and then boiled for 10 minutes.

✻ MAKING A FIRE ✻

Knowing how to start a fire without matches or a lighter is a useful survival skill. Attempting it can also be an entertaining way of passing the time. But before you actually set about lighting the fire it's essential to assemble all the different categories of material:

○ Tinder
○ Kindling
○ Twigs
○ Sticks

○ Logs

Don't make the mistake of starting the fire and then looking for material to feed it. You'll almost certainly fail.

HOW TO MAKE TINDER AND KINDLING

When you're making a fire under difficult conditions it's absolutely essential to have good, dry tinder and kindling.

○ Tinder is the finest, most easily ignited category of fire-starting material.

○ Kindling is the next size for adding to the fire.

Here are some possible sources of tinder:

○ Fibres from a piece of rope
○ Nests of rats, mice or birds
○ Dead, dry leaves
○ Dead, dry ferns, grass or pine needles
○ The inner bark from trees
○ Dried resin from where pines trees have been damaged

In all cases, prepare the tinder by shredding until you have a light, loose, well-ventilated pile, like teased-out cotton wool.

And here are some possible sources of kindling. When it's dry:

○ Find some dry twigs and crush them with a stone to split them into smaller fibres.

When it's wet:

○ With a knife, carve out some dry flakes of wood from inside a log or dead tree.

LIGHTING THE FIRE 🔥

Method 1 – the bow drill

For this method you will first need to prepare a bow, a drill, a drill holder, a fire block and some tinder.

The bow

Select a stick of springy wood about 3ft (1m) long and about three-quarters of an inch (2cm) thick. Attach a piece of string to one end, bend the wood to make a bow and tie off the string at the other end to hold it in shape. It will help to cut a couple of notches to stop the string from slipping.

The drill

For the drill, try to find a straight piece of dry, medium-hard wood about 1ft (30cm) long and about three-quarters of an inch (2cm) thick. You may need to shape it a little with a knife. Rather than being perfectly round a hexagonal sort of shape will give better grip to the bowstring. Make points at both ends.

The drill holder

You won't be able to hold the revolving drill with your bare hand so you need to make a drill holder. Essentially it's a small piece of wood, about the size and shape of half an orange, that you can comfortably grip with your hand. On the underside, lined up with the middle of your palm, make a hollow to accept one end of the drill. Ideally, lubricate the hollow with something like soap.

The fire block

The fire block should be of dry medium-hard wood such as elm or willow and about 8in (20cm) x 4in (10cm) x 1in (2.5cm). In the middle of it make a little hollow to accept the other end of the drill.

The tinder

Tinder is of vital importance for starting a fire. See the box above – *How to make tinder and kindling.*

To start the fire

Step 1. Place the fire block on the ground.

Step 2. Loop the bowstring around the drill. Put one end of the drill into the hollow in the fire block and fit the drill holder on to the upper end.

Step 3. Kneel on one leg with the foot of the other leg on the block to steady it. With the holder in your left hand and the bow in your right (if right handed) move the bow its full length backwards and forwards so as to spin the drill in the hollow.

Step 4. The drill will wear away a fine powder from the hollow in the fire block. It is this powder that will be the first to ignite due to the heat created by the friction of the drill.

Step 5. When the powder is smoking well, blow on it to raise the temperature.

Step 6. Add a little tinder and keep blowing. The tinder should burst into flames.

Step 7. Add more tinder and, when it's all burning, transfer the tinder to the fireplace.

Step 8. Gradually build up the fire.

Method 2 – the fire cord

In this method, instead of using a bow, you pull a length of stout cord backwards and forwards against a piece of wood to create heat by friction. Here's the way you do it:

Step 1. Find a suitable dead piece of wood about as thick as the circle made by a finger and thumb and about as long as a leg.

Step 2. Make a split at one end and hold it open with another small piece of wood or a stone.

Step 3. Take a stout thong roughly 3ft (1m) long, pass one end through the split, and tie the ends firmly to suitable pieces of wood to make handles.

Step 4. Place the split end of your piece of wood on a convenient stone about 1ft (30cm) high and kneel astride it, facing the split.

Step 5. Lightly pack some tinder into the V-end of the split.

Step 6. Holding the handles, pull your cord backwards and forwards against the upper side of the split so the heat generated by the friction can set light to the tinder (see the box above – *How to make tinder and kindling*).

Step 7. Once the tinder is smoking, blow on it to get a flame from which you can light some more tinder.

Step 8. Transfer the burning tinder to the fireplace and gradually build up the fire.

MAKING AN OVEN 🔥

Creating an 'oven' in the outdoors involves major 'engineering' works so you certainly shouldn't do it without permission unless it really is an emergency.

- Dig a circular pit about two feet across and two feet deep (60cm x 60cm).

- Lay a fire in the pit, with plenty of well-ventilated tinder and kindling at the bottom followed by increasingly larger layers of logs interspersed with solid-looking stones about the size of an orange.

○ Light the fire.

○ Eventually you'll have hot stones at the bottom of the pit – remove any leftover wood and still-glowing embers.

○ Wrap your food in foil or large leaves and arrange on the bed of hot stones with other hot stones around the edges.

○ Cover the food with a dense layer of small branches and leaves.

○ Push the earth from the hole back on top.

TIP ❁

○ If you want to steam your food, stand a straight stick in the middle of the oven as you fill it. When the earth has been pushed back extract the stick and pour water down the hole.

The heat of the stones will cook your food in an hour or two, which leaves you time to get on with something else, such as improving your emergency shelter.

❉ EMERGENCY SHELTER ❉

If you judge that, for whatever reason, it isn't going to be possible to get back to civilisation you're going to need to find or construct some form of emergency shelter. A little ingenuity can go a long way. First of all, look around for natural features you can make use of. A cave is an obvious one, but you might also be able to benefit from a rock overhang, a natural hollow or some dense bushes.

Here are some ideas.

Method 1 – the lean-to from saplings

If you can find three or so saplings growing close together in a line you can perhaps bend them over at an angle to create the basis of a sloping roof. For example, you might be able to attach cords to pull the tops down towards the ground and then anchor them.

⊘ If you have a plastic sheet you could trim away all the branches so you can then lay the sheet over the sapling supports.

⊘ If you don't have any sort of sheet, you'll need to 'fill in' the roof as much as possible by weaving in sticks at right angles and adding uprooted bushes and earth.

Method 2 – the tunnel from saplings

If you can find a group of saplings, see if it's possible to tie pairs together to create hoops. In other words, bend two saplings over towards one another so the tops overlap and then tie them with cord or reeds or whatever you can improvise. Then do the same with an adjacent pair, and another adjacent pair until you have the size you want. You can cover this tunnel shape with plastic or branches and earth.

Method 3 – the lean-to from branches

If you can find a suitable rock or wall or large fallen trunk you may be able to lean lengths of timber or branches against it to create a little crawl-in shelter.

Method 4 – the half-fallen tree

The idea of this is that you select a small tree and, at about shoulder height, set about cutting into the trunk sufficiently until you can push the upper part over. The aim is to have the top of the tree touching the ground in the direction the wind is coming from. Cut away the branches on the underside and weave them in with those on the top side to create as impermeable a 'roof' as possible.

Method 5 – the trench

If you can find some sort of natural trench – a dry ditch, a space between two stone walls – so much the better. If not, you'll have to get digging. Once you have a trench large enough to lie in, you can roof it with plastic sheeting or branches or timber.

Method 6 – the snow hole

Snow can seem a very hostile environment in which to be stranded but in fact it can be used in various ways to provide shelter.

- If you can dig a trench in it as in Method 5 you can roof it with branches and then with more snow on top. Use other branches as insulation in the bottom of the trench.

- Around the base of a tree you may find the snow has melted sufficiently to create a kind of shelter.

- If wind has banked up the snow it may be deep enough to excavate a cave.

Method 7 – when nature provides nothing

It's quite possible you could be caught out where there are no trees or bushes and where the ground is too hard or rocky to dig. In that case, move to the most sheltered spot and set about making yourself as protected as possible. For example:

- Put your legs inside your backpack.

- Pull your arms and hands inside your jacket.

- Put plastic bags on your hands or feet to form a 'vapour barrier' and then put your gloves and socks back on top.

- Make a rain hat from a plastic bag.

❋ GETTING HELP ❋

In the absence of a mobile phone (or coverage for one) you can try to attract attention in the following ways:

- A mirror. Tilt it rhythmically to make it clear that you're signalling intentionally. Better still, give three short flashes followed by three long ones followed by three short ones – Morse code for S.O.S.

TIPS ❧

You can improve your aim by scratching away a little circle in the silver backing of the mirror and using it as a 'sight'.

- Make a signal fire.

- Lay out spare clothing or rocks or pieces of wood in a regular pattern that will be noticeable from a distance; if you have enough, spell out S.O.S.

❋ EMERGENCY KIT ❋

If it's not too late and you're already halfway up a mountain in the fog, here's a basic list of essential emergency kit. It's worth packing this before you set out on the next leg of your expedition:

- Mobile phone
- Space blanket and orange plastic survival bag (available from outdoors shops)
- Pocket multi-tool
- String
- Map and compass
- Miniature flares
- Lighter
- Painkillers
- Water purification tablets
- Mirror (for signalling)
- Half a dozen small nuts and bolts for making repairs

THE WEATHER

It may seem that by far the easiest way of predicting the weather is to watch the weather forecast. And so you should, if you can. But if you're hiking in the wilderness for several days you won't be able to. What's more, the weather locally may be quite different from the overall picture, especially in the mountains.

CLOUDS

A knowledge of clouds is the key to making your own personal weather forecast. The names can sound quite technical but in fact there are only a few major cloud types and identifying them is quite easy.

Step 1. Decide whether the altitude is low, middle or high.

Step 2. Decide whether the shape is 'cotton wool,' uniform or wispy.

ALTITUDE

Get the altitude of the clouds first. It helps if there's some kind of reference point.

- **Low clouds** (below 2,000 metres). The summits of high mountains and even hills may be obscured.
- **Middle clouds** (2,000-8,000 metres). Mountain tops are clear.

Passenger jets have their wings and tails distinctly visible as they go in and out of the clouds,

○ **High clouds** (5,000-13,000 metres). Passenger jets at cruising altitude, the wings and tail barely visible, are still below the clouds.

SHAPE 🐚

Now that you've got the altitude, all you have to do is identify the shape in order to come up with the name of your cloud.

'Cotton wool' clouds

Clouds that are shaped like puffs of cotton wool are all *cumulus type* clouds.

Low

○ **Individual puffs** in an otherwise blue sky are known as **cumulus (Cu)**. If they grow and increase in number rain is likely.

○ **Puffs squashed together** so the sky looks like a mass of porridge with holes in it, are known as **stratocumulus (Sc)**. Rain follows.

Middle

○ **Puffs in lines** in an otherwise blue sky are known as **altocumulus (Ac)**. If the clouds in each line start joining together rain is on the way. If the tops turn into castles expect a thunderstorm.

High

○ **Puffs in orbit** giving the sky a stippled effect are known as **cirrocumulus (Cc)**. If they move fast the weather will deteriorate.

Low to high

⊙ **Cauliflowers** which begin *low* but tower up into the *middle* or even *high* cloud layer are known as **cumulonimbus (Cb)**. Angry-looking cumulonimbus clouds inevitably mean rain and thunderstorms.

'Uniform' cloud

Cloud which is a uniform grey, like a dirty ceiling, is *stratus type* cloud.

Low

⊙ **A dirty low ceiling** that obscures the tops of mountains and hills is known as **stratus (St)**. The air will feel damp and rain will almost certainly follow.

Middle

⊙ **A dirty middle-height ceiling** that produces the effect often described as 'watery sun' is known as **altostratus (As)**. If the clouds thicken rain is likely.

⊙ **A very dirty middle-height ceiling** that obscures the sun is known as **nimbostratus (Ns)**. It's usually associated with warmer weather and rain.

High

⊙ **A dirty high ceiling** that creates a halo round the sun or moon is known as **cirrostratus (Cs)**. It usually means bad weather within 48 hours.

'Wispy' cloud

○ **Tendrils** *high* up in an otherwise blue sky are known as **cirrus (Ci)** and are made of ice crystals. If you can see them moving strong winds are on the way within ten hours.

CLOUD MOVEMENT 🐾

Lower clouds don't necessarily move in the same direction as higher clouds. Stand with the lower clouds coming from behind you (in other words, with the wind on your back). Then:

○ If the higher clouds are moving in from your *right* the weather will be *all right*.

○ If the higher clouds are moving in from your left the weather will deteriorate.

○ If the higher clouds are moving either towards you or away from you the weather will stay the same.

✸ WIND ✸

THE BEAUFORT WIND FORCE SCALE 🐾

This was developed about 200 years ago by someone named, not surprisingly, Beaufort. The idea was to have a clear system for estimating the strength of the wind based on observation. The following table will enable you to judge the wind speed pretty accurately, whether you're on land or sea.

Force	Description	Knots	mph	km/h	Sea State	On Land
0	Calm	< 1	< 1	< 1	Sea like a mirror	Smoke rises vertically
1	Very Light	1–3	1–3	1–5	Ripples	Smoke drifts slowly
2	Light breeze	4–6	4–7	6–11	Small wavelets	Wind felt on face; leaves rustle
3	Gentle breeze	7–10	8–12	12–19	Scattered whitecaps	Leaves and light flags move
4	Moderate breeze	11–16	13–18	20–29	Numerous whitecaps	Paper blown about. Dust and small branches move
5	Fresh breeze	17–21	19–24	30–39	Many whitecaps; spray	Small trees sway
6	Strong breeze	22–27	25–31	40–50	Large waves	Large branches sway. Telephone wires 'whistle'
7	Near gale	28–33	32–38	51–61	Sea heaped up; white foam in streaks	Whole trees move. Difficult to walk
8	Gale	32–40	39–46	62–74	Foam blows	Small branches break off trees
9	Strong gale	41–47	47–54	75–87	Sea rolls	Slight structural damage eg slates off roofs
10	Storm	48–55	55–63	88–101	Sea surface white	Trees uprooted. Much structural damage
11	Violent storm	56–63	64–73	102–117	Exceptionally high waves	Widespread damage
12	Hurricane	> 64	>74	>119	Foam fills the air	Extreme damage

WIND ON THE COAST 🐌

On the coast, the wind over the sea and the wind over the land either converge or diverge:

○ Converging winds are stronger, with more cloud.

○ Diverging winds are lighter, with less cloud.

If you're on a small island you can use this phenomenon to decide which beaches to go to. Stand with your back to the wind and then:

○ The beaches to your *right* will be *all right* (there will be less wind and cloud).

○ The beaches to your *left* are best *left out* (there will be more wind and cloud).

Land heats up and cools down faster than sea, which creates the phenomenon of coastal breezes:

○ On a sunny morning air rising over the land sucks in cooler air over the sea causing an *onshore* breeze.

○ At night air rising over the sea sucks in cooler air from over the land causing an *offshore* breeze.

○ If there are sea cliffs or mountains behind the coast, cold air descending from the summits in the early hours can cause *katabatic winds* which, augmenting the offshore breeze, can be extremely violent.

✻ PRESSURE ✻

In order to follow what's happening with the atmospheric pressure you'll need a portable barometer, nowadays cheaply available and often incorporated into watches.

Atmospheric pressure is measured in millibars (mb). At sea level, pressure ranges from 950mb up to 1050mb and 'normal' pressure is considered to be around 1013mb in England.

Rule of thumb ─○

Pressure falls about 1mb for every 10 metres of altitude. In other words, if the pressure was 1013mb in Caernarfon Bay it would be around 913mb on top of nearby Mount Snowdon (1,085 metres).

HIGH PRESSURE

- If the pressure at the centre of a weather system is higher than at the edges then the pressure is said to be 'high'.

- A high is also known as an anti-cyclone.

- In a high the wind circulates clockwise (in the northern hemisphere).

- In a high the air is *descending* which means the air warms up and the clouds disappear.

LOW PRESSURE

- If the pressure at the centre of a weather system is lower than at the edges then the pressure is said to be 'low'.

- A low is also known as a depression.

- In a low the wind circulates anticlockwise (in the northern hemisphere).

○ In a low the air is *rising* which means the air cools down and clouds appear.

CHANGING PRESSURE

○ Pressure steady at around 1013mb at sea level, or rising slowly, suggests good weather.

○ A change of 5mb in three hours suggests a strong breeze.

○ A change of 8mb in three hours suggests a gale.

○ A slow fall in pressure suggests rain.

❋ PREDICTING THE WEATHER ❋

The weather in Britain is generally driven by low pressure systems that move across the country in a north-easterly direction. These systems tend to follow a particular five-step sequence which looks like this:

1 Cold air with stratocumulus and cumulus and *clear visibility*.

2 *Warm front* with cirrus, cirrostratus, altostratus, nimbostratus and *RAIN*.

3 Warm air with stratocumulus and stratus and *poor visibility*.

4 Cumulonimbus with *RAIN*.

5 *Cold front* with cumulus and *RAIN*.

1 Cold air with stratocumulus and cumulus and *clear visibility*.

2 *Warm front* . . .

Of course, this is a typical pattern but in reality things may not work out quite like that. However, by observing the clouds, visibility, temperature and rain you should be able to work out which of the five steps you're on and predict which steps will follow.

WEATHER LORE

There's a lot of folklore associated with the weather and quite a lot of it is *true*, including the following:

Sunrise

○ If you can see the sun coming up on the horizon expect good weather.

○ If the sun rises above a bank of cloud expect wind.

○ If the sky is red at sunrise and clouds tower up later expect rain.

○ If the sky is purple at dawn expect storms.

Sunset

○ If the sky is light red at sunset expect good weather.

○ If the sky is greenish, pale yellow, dark red or purple at sunset expect rain.

○ If the sky is bright yellow at sunset expect wind.

Moon

○ If you can see the full moon rising a silvery-white expect good weather.

○ If you can see the full moon rising a pale yellow expect rain.

○ If the moon looks red expect wind.

Rings round the sun or moon

○ A large ring or halo round the sun or moon means rain.

○ The larger the halo the more imminent the rain.

○ The halo may be open on the side the rain will be coming from.

COASTLINE

Nowhere in Britain is more than about 75 miles from the coast which means that the pleasures of a little beachcombing are never far away.

�֎ SEASHELLS �֎

Shells are the armour of marine molluscs. They're made mostly of calcium carbonate, which is secreted by the creature's mantle, and grow as the mollusc grows.

In environmental terms, collecting the shells of dead marine molluscs is perfectly benign. They're destined to be reduced to fine sand anyway. But:

❂ Make sure the shells you take for your collection are empty.

Since shells grow, the sizes mentioned here should be treated only as a very rough guide to help identification.

Half shells

❂ **Limpets**. Small, shallow and crudely circular shells (like one castanet) coming to a point in the middle from which lines radiate out. Usually white to brown but occasionally red.

Hinged shells (bivalves)

❂ **Cockles**. These look like small scallop shells (see below), usually around the size of a £2 coin but reaching a maximum of about 2.5in/6cm. Often the two halves are found still joined together. Lines radiate out from the hinge. Normally whitish.

○ **Mussels**. These are large, metallic-blue shells, usually with a handsome sheen of mother-of-pearl inside. They range from around 1in/2.5cm up to as much as 8in/20cm and, when alive, grow in clusters.

○ **Clams**. Somewhat oval shells up to about 5in/7.5cm across, grey or brown, and fairly delicate with fine lines.

○ **Scallops**. These large, handsome shells are the emblem of the Shell oil company, reaching a size of about 4in/10cm. White to reddish brown. One shell is flat and the other is convex.

○ **Oysters**. Wild oysters are rare in UK waters nowadays. The shells are sometimes circular, more often like squashed circles, very thick and flaking. They usually reach a size of about 4in/10cm.

○ **Razor shells**. As the name implies, these are shaped somewhat like the blade of a cut-throat razor and grow to a length of around 4in/10cm.

Spiral shells

○ **Periwinkle (often shortened to winkle)**. Small, spiral shell coming to a point and with a maximum length of about 1in/2.5cm. Usually greyish and banded.

○ **Flat periwinkle**. More like the shell of a snail and very varied. Green shells dominate on sheltered coasts while exposed shores tend to produce brown shells. But they can also be mottled or even striped in yellow, orange or red.

- **Whelk**. Spiral shell coming to a point, as with periwinkle, but much larger (usually around 4in/10cm and very thick).

- **Needle whelk**. Tiny, narrow, pretty spirals that range from white through fawn to red.

- **Dogwhelk**. Similar to whelk and usually grey but can be striped. It's identified by a groove on the underside of the shell.

- **Toothed top shell**. Shaped something like an old-fashioned wooden spinning top with only a few whorls and often brightly coloured. Grow up to about 1.25in/3cm.

- **Acteon tornatilis** (no English name). Handsome pink-banded shell.

TIP ❁

It's easy to see inside the shell of a dead bivalve but not inside spiral shells which can be even more fascinating. As the mollusc grows so it creates larger and larger chambers and as it does so it seals off the smaller chambers that it's evacuated behind it. These become buoyancy chambers. In order to expose this fantastic structure, take hold of a spiral shell wearing a pair of gloves and rub one spot against a sheet of coarse sandpaper until a sufficiently large viewing hole is worn away.

❁ LIFE ON THE SHORE ❁

It's fun to collect beautiful shells. But it's also interesting to watch the live molluscs. They may seem as if they never move but in fact they do:

- At the very edge of the low-tide line on sandy shores watch for the razor shells. Walk very softly. As you approach you'll see them suddenly disappear into the sand.

- Bivalve molluscs pull themselves into the sand by their feet. When the tide comes in they extend siphons into the water, one to take in plankton rich water the other to eject the waste.

- Most molluscs hide when the tide goes out but toothed top shells often remain out on the rocks.

- Limpets also remain visible. They feed on algae at high tide, leaving a mucus trail behind them on the rock. After feeding, a limpet follows the trail back to the 'home-scar' which it created by a mixture of chemical action and abrasion and reattaches itself exactly as before.

- You may see a mussel with a dogwhelk attached. The dog-whelk is one of the most voracious predators on the shore. It drills into the mussel's shell over a period of up to a week in order to get at the flesh inside.

Small holes in the mud can have various explanations including:

- Star-like markings – **ragworm**.

- Two holes a few inches apart with a worm cast at one end – **lugworm** (which lives in a U-shaped burrow).

❊ ROCK POOLS ❊

CRABS 🦀

Crabs are among the best-known inhabitants of the shore. All of them have 10 legs, of which two have developed as powerful claws. They include:

- **Shore crab** – the one you're most likely to see, ranging from tiny to the size of a hand; usually mottled brown but occasion-ally orange and even green.

- **Edible crab** – oval shell with a pie-crust edge; reddish.

- **Hairy crab** – similar to edible crab but covered in hair and the two claws are different sizes.

- **Velvet swimming crab** – a fine, dense covering of hair on the shell gives this crab its name; bright red eyes; extremely powerful nip.

- **Sandy swimming crab** – sandy or orange coloured and a good swimmer.

- **Masked crab** – instead of walking sideways this burrows backwards into the sand; its two antennae are modified into a breathing tube.

- **Pea crab** – the male is the size of a pea, brown and swims; the female is twice the size, yellow with a red spot, and lives inside the shell of a live mussel.

- **Spider crabs** – a family of crabs with long, thin legs. The short-legged has a shell measuring a maximum of about 1in/2.5cm; the long-legged resembles a Daddy Long-legs; the spiny spider crab can grow to a shell length of 7in/18cm.

- **Hermit crabs** – at least 15 species in British waters. They live inside the shells of dead molluscs. Small ones live in periwinkle shells, larger ones in whelk shells. If you see a mollusc *crawling* along the floor of a rock pool then it's a hermit crab.

- **Porcelain crabs** – not true crabs but resemble them. The hairy porcelain crab is about the size of a 10p coin and its two large claws are fringed with hair. The long-clawed porcelain crab is about the size of a 5p coin. Both species have eight visible legs, including the claws, as against 10 for true crabs.

Rule of thumb —○

Sometimes you may find the shell of a crab. It doesn't mean the crab is dead because crabs shed their shells as they grow. If you see holes where the eyes should be you can tell the crab has moulted.

SOME OTHER CREATURES 🦐

○ **Sea anemones** – look like flowers but are animals and can move around either by creeping or by inflating and letting the water carry them. They consist of a column with a mouth surrounded by tentacles containing sting capsules.

○ **Sea cucumbers** – are the vacuum cleaners of the underwater world. Up to about 1ft/30cm long, cylindrical and brown, they 'eat' the sand, digest any food particles and eject clean sand.

○ **Lobsters** – are best known as an exotic food but can be seen in all their live glory on sandy or muddy shorelines or hiding under a ledge or in a burrow under rocks. They have two big front pincer claws and two feelers. Generally the lobster will amble slowly across the sea bed but if in danger will flee backwards by curling and uncurling the abdomen. They look similar to the smaller **Crawfish** (also known as crayfish, especially in the US) but these live in fresh water.

○ **Squat lobsters** – aren't true lobsters but look like them; reddish and blueish, they reach a maximum of 7in/17.5cm long.

○ **Starfish** – typically have five arms and are generally orange although in the case of the greenish cushion star, growing to about 2.5"/6cm, the arms are not very distinct.

○ **Jellyfish** – are well-known for their ethereal beauty. Not all species can sting humans but those that do include the huge, reddish Lion's Mane, the Compass, the Blue and the Mauve Stinger. The Portuguese Man o' War can also sting but it's technically a colonial hydrozoan, not a jellyfish. The By-the-wind Sailor, another colonial hydrozoan, is often seen washed up in thousands.

TIP ❀

Some jellyfish stings are nothing worse than nettle stings. But others, especially from the Mauve Stinger, can be serious. Even detached tentacles can hurt. Wash the area with fresh water immediately and apply an ice-pack for 15 minutes. An antihistamine cream may help. If blisters develop consult a doctor.

Rule of thumb —O

When watching life on the shore and in rock pools:

❂ Always replace rocks turned over exactly as they were.
❂ Cause the minimum of disturbance.

❀ SEMI-PRECIOUS STONES ❀

Beaches are great places to hunt for semi-precious stones and even 'precious' stones. But don't get too excited. Although you might just find sapphires on Mull and topaz crystals on Arran and the beaches of Aberdeenshire and Argyll, they're too flawed to be of any commercial value.

Rule of thumb ─○

Is it quartz or glass? Most semi-precious stones are varieties of quartz. But weathered quartz and weathered glass cam sometimes look very similar:

○ Quartz is extremely hard and scratches less easily than glass.

○ When struck hard by something like a knife blade in a darkened room quartz will spark and give off a slight vegetable smell; glass will not.

SOME SEMI-PRECIOUS STONES AND WHERE TO FIND THEM

○ **Amber** – Technically not a stone but fossil resin. Pale yellow through to deep burnt orange. Soft and easily scratched. Light, brittle and burns with a noticeable smell. A well-known test for amber is its static electricity. Tear up small pieces of paper and rub a piece of amber vigorously on your sleeve. It will attract the paper to it. Can be found on UK beaches between Yorkshire and Essex.

○ **Amethyst** – translucent, light purple or violet. Cornish beaches and east coast of Scotland.

○ **Banded agate** – translucent with curved stripes of different colours. Best hunting grounds are the Scottish coasts (agates banded with pink and white are known as Scotch pebbles) and beaches in eastern England and Cornwall.

○ **Chalcedony** – translucent but with a hint of smokiness, pale blue-grey to light brown with a bubble-like surface. Found on beaches in Scotland, eastern England and southern England.

○ **Jasper** – opaque and dull red through to brown or yellowish green. Grains of clay can easily been seen with a magnifying glass. Jasper is easily marked with a knife.

○ **Jet** – not a quartz but derived from vegetable matter. Related to coal but harder and glossy. The best examples are 'jet' black and opaque although you can find browner, softer examples. The only site to find jet in the UK is Whitby on the Yorkshire coast.

TIP ❧

To test for jet, scrape off any weathering and verify that it is black and shiny underneath. Jet is lighter than glass. Hold a flame to the edge and it will burn greenish and smell slightly tarry.

○ **Onyx** – like agate but rather than curved banding the stripes of colour are straight.

TIP ❧

Is it Agate/Onyx or Schist/Slate? Pebbles of schist or slate can sometimes look like agate and onyx because of their banding, but a knife won't scratch agate or onyx whereas it will scratch schist and slate.

○ **Rose quartz** – opaque and pink to salmon coloured. Carnelian Bay, Scarborough.

○ **Yellow quartz** – translucent, pale yellow to gold. Bridlington Bay, near Flamborough Head and Hornsea Beach in east Yorkshire.

○ **Smokey quartz** – (also known as Cairngorm as it comes from the Cairngorm Mountains of Scotland). Translucent but with a hint of smokiness and varying from yellow through deep orange to dark brown. Can be found on the beaches of east Scotland and the east coast of England.

❀ WATER SAFETY ❀

IS IT SAFE TO SWIM OR PADDLE? 🐚

The strength of the sea should never be underestimated. Even knee-deep water can be enough to sweep an adult away if there's a powerful surf:

○ Don't swim if you can see there's a sewer outfall nearby.

○ Beware of shingle – the surf can pull it out from under you like a carpet and make you fall.

○ If the beach shelves steeply it would be prudent to assume it continues at least at the same angle underwater. Don't let children or weak swimmers go in.

○ Avoid headlands, especially three hours after or before high/low water when tidal streams will be at their fiercest.

○ If you're in the slightest doubt, don't go in.

○ Don't even get near during a storm – a freak wave might drag you in.

CUT OFF BY THE TIDE 🐚

It can be great fun to walk or swim at low tide to beaches or sandbanks or rocks that are covered at high tide. But it's also extremely hazardous:

- Never do such a thing without being absolutely certain of how long you can safely stay before returning.

- Make sure you're absolutely certain of the topography.

- Never go if there's even the slightest chance of mist or fog.

- Keep a close eye on the state of the water because unusual conditions may cause the tide to turn earlier than expected.

- If you don't understand the tides take a look at the chapter on *Boats*.

If you are cut off by an incoming tide you're in potentially serious trouble. It's impossible to give hard and fast rules because every situation is different. But here are some possibilities:

- If you know which way the tide is advancing and you're on, for example, a long sandbank, you may be able to get ahead of the incoming tide and reach safety.

- If there's no way of escape, move to the highest ground and signal for help (see *Survival skills*).

- If you're cut off but on land which is in no danger of being submerged then it's a question of surviving the weather until the tide recedes again (see *Survival skills*).

- If you're cut off on land which will be submerged then, if all else fails, it's a question of surviving in the water until help arrives or you can reach safety.

SEA SURVIVAL

The sea around Britain generally varies from around 60°F (16°C) down to 40°F (4°C). Fresh water may even get close to freezing. At the lower temperatures a swimmer would become unconscious in less than 15 minutes.

Survival times in water

Temperature	Loss of consciousness	Death
Just above freezing	Under 15 minutes	30 minutes
Up to 40°F/4°C	15-30 minutes	30-90 minutes
40°F/4°C–50°F/10°C	30-60 minutes	1-3 hours
50°F/10°C–60° F/16°C	1-2 hours	1-6 hours

The above figures are for an adult wearing only a swimming costume. Note that children generally lose body heat more quickly.

You can improve your survival chances by:

● Keeping on some clothing and minimising movement to conserve body heat.

● Finding a buoyancy aid such as a lump of driftwood or creating one from, for example, an inflated plastic bag.

Boats

As Ratty put it in *The Wind in the Willows*, there is absolutely nothing half so much worth doing as simply messing about in boats. But messing about in boats can be dangerous unless you've had proper instruction. This section is a reminder of some of the key points.

❋ GLOSSARY ❋

To kick off with here's a quick glossary of some of those nautical terms. So if someone tells you to haul in a sheet you'll know what they're talking about:

Aft – near or towards the stern or back.

Amidships – the centre part of the boat.

Astern – going backwards.

Bow – the pointed bit, the sharp end, the front.

Cable – the chain or warp (rope) attached to the anchor.

Close-hauled – sailing as close as possible to where the wind is coming from.

Cutter – sailing boat with one mast, one mainsail and two head-sails.

Fender – something to prevent damage when alongside a quay or another boat.

Go about – to change from one tack to another on a sailing boat.

Gaff cutter – sailing boat with one mast, a mainsail divided into two parts, and two headsails.

Headsail – any sail set forward of the mast.

Ketch – a sailing boat with a second, small mast behind the first.

Port – the left side of the boat when looking forward.

Port tack – sailing with the wind on the port side.

Schooner – a sailing boat with two masts, of which the one aft is the tallest.

Sheet – a rope controlling a sail.

Sloop – sailing boat with one mast, one mainsail and one headsail.

Starboard – the right side of the boat when looking forward.

Starboard tack – sailing with the wind on the starboard side.

Stern – the back.

Tacking – sailing to windward, with the wind alternately on one side and then the other.

Warp – a rope attached to an anchor.

Yawl – a sailing boat with a second, small mast behind the first, from which the sail protrudes beyond the stern.

✳ THE BASICS ✳

BEFORE SETTING OFF

⊙ Tell someone where you're going and what time you plan to be back.

⊙ Make sure the boat is appropriately equipped. If it's a small boat powered by an outboard, for example, are there oars in case the engine packs up? Is there an anchor to stop the boat drifting onto the rocks? Is there a radio or do you have a mobile phone? Are there signal flares?

⊙ Ideally, everybody on board should know how to handle the boat. As a minimum, two people should know because if the 'skipper' falls in everyone faces disaster.

⊙ Everyone should wear a life jacket.

Rule of thumb ⊸○
When getting into a small boat always try to step into the middle, otherwise you may tip it up.

GETTING UNDER WAY 🐚

If your boat is tied to, say, bollards or rings, it will be more convenient to use slip ropes when it's time to get away. That way, nobody has to be on the quayside to untie the boat:

⊙ Untie the bow and stern lines and rearrange them as slip ropes. In other words they should run from the boat to the bollard or ring and back to the boat again.

⊙ Remove any other lines.

○ To prevent jamming as you move away slip ropes should be passed:
  – *Up* through rings which lie horizontally on top of a quay.
  – *Down* through rings which hang *down*.

○ Pull the slip ropes inboard rapidly – don't let them foul the propeller.

Launching from a beach

If you're launching a small boat from the beach be sure the conditions are sufficiently calm. How you go about it depends on several factors. The first rule is to make sure the boat doesn't get damaged as it's lifted and then dropped by the waves:

○ Any centreboard, rudder or outboard should be in the raised position.

○ A boat with a heavy outboard needs to be launched stern first on its trailer.

○ A light boat with a small outboard can be launched and the outboard attached in the water.

○ An inflatable should never be dragged but carried or launched from a trailer, otherwise the fabric could be damaged.

Getting the boat moving

As soon as the water at the stern is deep enough, and with the bows afloat, the motor can then be lowered and started. It may be possible for some passengers to step in over the bows at this point or it may be necessary for the coxswain (the 'driver') to urgently reverse the boat away from the beach to avoid damage (in which case the passengers are going to get a bit wet as they board).

Normally one person remains in the water until the boat is ready to leave and then climbs in over the side.

Rule of thumb —○

The height of the waves at the beach is related to the depth of the water.

❂ The waves will be at their smallest around high tide.
❂ The waves will be at their largest around low tide.

If you launch at high water and return at low water you may find the conditions much more difficult, even though the wind remains the same.

Keeping the boat level

Under way the boat should be fairly level and the outboard, if there is one, should be going down vertically into the water, not at an angle. For example, with two people aboard, one may have to sit at the stern controlling the outboard and the other may therefore need to sit amidships, to prevent the bows lifting.

Deciding where to sit

In the case of a sailing dinghy, the crew will have to arrange themselves so as to keep the mast as vertical as possible. In a strong wind, that means everyone will be sitting on the windward side. The crew should be ready to move more inboard if the wind drops. When going about (moving onto the opposite tack) the crew will first have to move inboard and then, *only when the boom has swung over*, across to the opposite side of the boat. Moving across too soon will tip the boat up.

WHICH WAY TO TURN
(THE PROPELLER EFFECT) 🐾

A boat with an inboard engine and single screw will always turn more easily in one direction than another, using forward and reverse, due to the effect of the propeller 'walking' the stern of the boat. Every boat is different, but in general, while the prop has little effect as the boat moves ahead, it has a significant effect astern.

Therefore, in a confined space such as a marina:

○ If you have a right-handed screw, turn to starboard.
○ If you have a left-handed screw, turn to port.

How will you know which way the prop turns?

Run the engine *astern* while the boat is tied up and watch for the turbulence. If the turbulence is on the starboard (right) side, the stern will move to port (left) which means you have a so-called 'right-handed' screw (and should therefore turn to starboard).

✹ BUOYS ✹

If you're starting off from a harbour or estuary you may find there's a system of red and green buoys to mark the channel you should be following. By convention, however, the directions are all taken in terms of a boat entering.

The basic principle is that:

○ When *entering* a harbour or river, the red buoys must be on your port side and the green buoys must be on your starboard side. You may find it helpful to remember port wine = red = port (left) side; or *is there any red port left?*

○ When *leaving* a harbour or river, the red buoys must be on your starboard side and the green buoys must be on your port side.

Of course, in major shipping lanes these channels are laid out with big ships in mind. *Small boats should be at the very edge of the channel or even outside the channel, depending on the depths.* You'll find the depths marked on a chart.

○ If a buoy is painted red but with a green band, it means the preferred channel is to starboard of the buoy (so you keep the buoy on your port side).

○ If a buoy is painted green but with a red band, it means the preferred channel is to port of the buoy (so you keep the buoy on your starboard side).

You may also see:

○ Red and black buoys – mark dangerous spots.

○ Red and white buoys – mark safe water.

○ Yellow and black buoys – known as cardinal marks, they also indicate hazards but rather than being placed on the hazard they're at a distance from it. On top there will be two black cones:

  – If both black cones point up, pass to the north.

  – If both black cones point down, pass to the south.

  – If the cones point away from one another (top up, bottom down) pass to the east. Memory trick – the cones make the shape of an *E*gg for *E*ast.

  – If the cones point at one another (top down, bottom up) pass to the west. Memory trick – the cones make the shape of a *W*ineglass for *W*est.

❋ RIGHT OF WAY ❋

The right of way rules are quite complicated. The most important things to remember are:

⊘ Keep a look out at all times.

⊘ Large boats can't change direction very quickly; in a small boat you'll simply have to keep out of the way in *all* circumstances.

⊘ It's better to take evasive action long before right of way even becomes an issue.

HOW CAN YOU TELL IF THERE'S A CHANCE OF COLLISION? 🦶

Take compass bearings of the 'problem' boat at intervals. If the bearing doesn't change then you're heading for a collision.

TO AVOID A COLLISION 🦶

Make a positive course alteration of about 40 degrees with at least five minutes to spare.

The key collision rules are:

⊘ In a narrow channel you must keep to the starboard side so you will pass oncoming boats port side to port side.

⊘ When crossing a channel do so at right angles.

⊘ When two sailing boats are approaching one another on opposite tacks the boat on the starboard tack has right of way.

⊘ When two sailing boats are approaching one another on the same tack the downwind boat has right of way.

❂ When two boats under power are approaching one another head on *both* should alter course to starboard.

❂ When two boats under power are approaching one another on different courses, the one which has the other on her starboard side keeps clear.

❂ When a boat under power and a boat under sail are at risk of collision the boat under power must give way *except when the boat under power is restricted in its ability to manoeuvre.*

❂ An overtaking boat must keep clear of the boat being over-taken.

SOUND SIGNALS

A power-driven boat may make signals on a whistle or siren:

❂ One short blast means 'I am altering course to starboard'.

❂ Two short blasts mean 'I am altering course to port'.

Here's a little seaman's ditty that's worth remembering:

> Here lies the body of Michael O'Day
> Who died maintaining the right of way;
> He was right, dead right, as he sailed along,
> But he's just as dead as if he'd been wrong.

✱ TIDES ✱

Tides are caused by the attraction of the sun and moon, but the power of the moon is about two-and-a-half times stronger than that of the sun.

❂ There are two high tides and two low tides every day.

- Successive high or low tides will be approximately 12 hours 27 minutes apart.

- A particular tide will be 54 minutes later than the previous day. So if morning high tide is at 10.00 today, it will be at 10.54 tomorrow.

SPRING AND NEAP TIDES

So-called 'spring' tides do not occur in the spring. In fact, they occur roughly twice a month:

Spring tides result when the moon and sun work together – the tidal range is at its greatest so the water reaches both its maximum and minimum depths.

Neap tides result when the moon and sun work at right angles to one another – the tidal range is at its smallest.

Rule of thumb —○

Because of a time lag spring tides don't occur precisely at new and full moons, but about 36 hours afterwards.

However, there *are* unusually high tides in the spring. They're called **equinoctial tides** and they're caused by the sun and moon being particularly closely aligned. They also occur again in September. **Solstice tides**, when the combined effect of the sun and moon is at its weakest, occur in June and December.

TIDAL STREAMS

Tides create *tidal streams* (whereas *currents* are produced by meteorological conditions). Tidal streams can be extremely power-ful in some places, especially in narrow channels and around headlands. In order to avoid the most dangerous tidal streams (or to calculate by how much the water will go up or down at any given time) it's important to know **The Twelfths Rule**:

1st hour	1/12 of range
2nd hour	2/12 of range
3rd hour	3/12 of range
4th hour	3/12 of range
5th hour	2/12 of range
6th hour	1/12 of range

It may help you to remember 1, 2, 3, 3, 2, 1.

In other words, in the first hour after high or low water the depth will only change by one-twelfth of the total and the tidal stream will be weak. But in the third and fourth hours the rate of change will be at its maximum and the tidal stream will be at its most powerful.

PROBLEMS

MAN OVERBOARD

Man overboard is one of the most dangerous situations. Work out in advance what you'll do if it happens. How will the person get back into the boat, for example? A small boat can easily be upset by someone trying to climb in over the side – it may be better to get in over the bow or stern. If it's a larger boat, is there a ladder?

Here are some man overboard tips:

- If there's a GPS on board, press the MOB (man overboard) button immediately; the location will then be locked into the memory and the course back will be given.

○ If there's no GPS, one crew member should do nothing other than point at the person in the water.

○ Throw a lifebuoy into the water at once and other floating objects at intervals to mark the way back to the person in the water. Of course, they'll all be drifting in the wind and current but they'll be a help.

○ When close to the person it may help to deploy a flotation line – but make sure it can't foul the propeller.

○ Stop the boat at right-angles to the person in the water and upwind, and with the engine in neutral to make sure the propeller doesn't cause an injury. (The reason is that the boat will be blown faster than the person in the water; if the boat was downwind you'd be separated before you could get the person on board.)

○ If a second person has to get into the water to help, he or she should be attached to the boat by a safety line.

DISTRESS SIGNALS 🕯️

If you're in distress here are some of the ways you can signal for help:

○ Continuously sound the foghorn.

○ Fire red parachute flares, red hand flares or red stars.

○ Repeatedly raise and lower your outstretched arms.

○ Send an SOS signal by any method at all (radio, torchlight etc) using the Morse Code:

··· _ _ _ ···

Of course, if you have a mobile phone you can call the Coastguard (see Emergency Numbers at the back of the book) and if you have a VHF radio you can put out a Mayday.

✳ NAVIGATING ✳

A car always goes where you point it. On water, things are very different. You seldom point the boat where you want it to go because wind, tide and current could push you well to, say, starboard (the right). In which case, you'd have to aim much more to port (the left). The effect is particularly strong for sailing boats. But how can you tell how much to steer away from where you actually want to go? You can get a clue by:

❂ Watching the wake and comparing it with the fore-and-aft line of the boat.

For example, if there's a difference of 15 degrees between the wake and the boat then you need to point the boat 15 degrees more to windward. However, the boat can also be moved by currents. A way of allowing for both effects is to find a landmark behind the place you're aiming for and in a straight line with it. If the two points don't remain 'in register' you're being pushed off course:

❂ If the landmark moves out to the right, you need to steer more to port (the left).

❂ If the landmark moves out to the left, you need to steer more to starboard (the right).

✳ ANCHORING ✳

An anchor only digs itself into the sea bed when it is pulled more or less horizontally by its cable. In other words, if the anchor chain or warp is the same as the depth of the water the pull will be vertical and the anchor will not hold. The minimum length therefore is:

○ Chain – at least three times the maximum depth of the water.

○ Warp (rope) – at least five times the maximum depth of the water.

Note that warp should never be connected directly to an anchor. There should always be at least two fathoms (12 feet) of chain to provide some weight and prevent the warp chafing against rocks on the seabed.

HOW TO ANCHOR

The usual procedure for anchoring a boat is to head into the wind (or current, if its effect is more powerful), drop the anchor and then let the boat fall back, paying out the right amount of cable as you go. If there's very little wind or current you'll have to 'set' the anchor by reversing.

Make sure you won't foul someone else's anchor cable or collide with another boat. Remember:

○ A boat will always try to face the wind when there's no current.

○ A boat will always try to face the current when there's no wind.

○ When there's both wind and current each boat will respond according to how much is above the water and how much is below the water.

This is why boats of different designs shouldn't be at anchor or on swinging moorings close together.

KNOTS

Every outdoors person needs to know how to tie a few knots.

When practising a knot it's best to use soft rope with a woven outer sheath rather than thin string because it's much easier to see what you're doing – and to untie the knot again afterwards. Something with a diameter of about 10mm is ideal.

�֎ GENERAL KNOTS �֎

THE FIGURE OF EIGHT ✤

This is an easy one to kick off with. It takes its name from its shape which is, indeed, a figure of eight. It's normally made in the end of a rope to make a thick 'stopper' so tie the other end of the rope to, say, a chair leg and then forget about it. Let's say, for example, that on a boat a rope passes through a pulley. A figure of eight might be tied in the end so that, if the rope was accidentally released or dropped, the 'stopper' would prevent it from passing back through the pulley.

1 Make a loop by passing the rope *over* itself, about 1ft (30cm) back from the tip/free end.

2 Now pass the free end of the rope *under* the standing part, a little further towards the tied-off end. You should now have two loops looking like a figure of eight.

3 Take the free end and feed it *downwards* through the first loop you made. Pull tight.

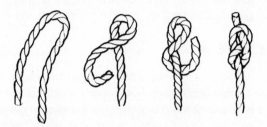

THE SHEET BEND AND THE DOUBLE SHEET BEND

This is the knot for tying two cords together – or two ends of the same cord to make a loop. The doubled version adds extra strength. It's similar to the well-known reef or square knot but is far more secure.

1 Take the first cord and turn the last, say, 10 cm back to make a long-sided U-shape.

2 Take the second cord and pass it up the middle of the U, out over the right-hand prong, round the back and then – this is the cunning part – *under* itself. Pull tight.

THE DOUBLE VARIATION ✍

Simply pass the second cord not once but twice around the U before jamming it under itself.

THE BOWLINE ✍

This is probably the most useful knot you could ever learn. One of its most famous applications is in creating a non-tightening loop around your own or somebody else's waist to assist in a rescue. It's also an excellent way of creating a loop that can be untied again fairly easily, even after being subject to quite a lot of pressure. To avoid confusion, tie one end of your rope to a chair leg or something like that; the rope coming from the chair leg is then known as the 'standing part'.

1 Make a *small* loop by passing the rope *over* itself, about 2ft (60cm) back from the tip/free end. To avoid confusion later we're going to call this first loop 'the rabbit hole'.

2 Now take the tip/free end and pass it *up* through 'the rabbit hole'. By so doing you've now created a second, much bigger loop. This second loop is the one that we're actually interested in creating. We're now going to fix this second loop by completing the knot.

3 Pass the tip/free end *under* the standing part, curl it around and push it *down* through 'the rabbit hole'. Some people like to remember the sequence like this. The tip (the rabbit) comes out of 'the rabbit hole', hops around the tree (the standing part) and then pops down 'the rabbit hole' again. Pull the knot tight while keeping the big loop the size you want it.

If you want a bigger loop then you simply make your 'rabbit hole' further back. If you want it smaller than you make your 'rabbit hole' nearer the tip of the rope.

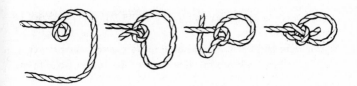

Tying a bowline round your own waist

Once you can tie the bowline as described above it's a good idea to practise tying bowlines in the dark, to other people and to yourself. You never know when you might desperately need it. So let's imagine you fell over a cliff. You're not seriously hurt but you can't climb up again. A rescuer throws down a rope's end. This is what you do:

1 Pass the rope around your back from your left side to your right side and hold it in place between your upper right arm and your side.

2 Make 'the rabbit hole' in the standing part as follows. Grasp the 'standing part' of the rope (the part that's leading from the rescuers) with the fingers of your left hand. Now also grasp the rope with

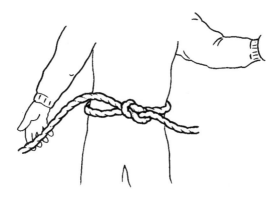

the fingers of your right hand, but about 6in (15cm) closer to your body. Twist the rope with the thumb and fingers of your right hand at the same time moving your hands closer to one another. Hey presto! The loop of the 'rabbit hole' forms itself.

3 Pass the tip/free end up through 'the rabbit hole' round the standing part and back down through 'the rabbit hole' again. Pull tight.

THE PRUSIK KNOT

This is another knot to get you out of a tight spot. Let's say there's a rope hanging down but no one at the top of it strong enough to haul you up. Your only chance is to climb it. But how?

Stage 1. Make some slings

You'll need a sling or 'Prusik loop' for each foot, made from strong cord significantly thinner than the rope you're going to climb – say about 5mm. It's a good idea to have a third, smaller, sling passing around you under your arms for stability.

1 Cut two lengths of cord, each about 12ft (4m) long, and a third about 6ft (2m) long.

2 Make the cords into three Prusik loops by joining each pair of ends using sheet bends (see above).

Stage 2. Attach the slings to the rope

This is really very simple.

1 Take hold of your Prusik loop in your right hand, exactly where you've tied the sheet bend. Pass the far side of the Prusik loop

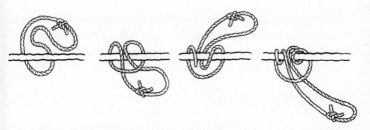

behind the rope you're going to climb and take hold of that (diametrically opposite) part in your left hand.

2 Now pass the sheet bend around the front of the rope, *inside* the loop of cord you're holding in your left hand, right round the climbing rope and through the loop in your left hand a second time.

3 Transfer the sheet bend to your left hand and pull to tighten the Prusik loop around the climbing rope.

4 Repeat the procedure with the second Prusik loop and the shorter, third Prusik loop which should be above the other two.

5 You've now got three Prusik loops which can be slid along the rope when they're not under pressure but which will tighten and grip the rope when you put your weight on them.

Stage 3. Climb the rope

This isn't at all simple but it could be a life saver.

1 Get the shorter Prusik loop over your head and under your arms. This is for stability.

2 Climb the rope by standing in one Prusik loop and advancing the other sufficiently so that you can step up into it, as if climbing a rope ladder. You'll also have to keep moving the smaller 'stability' loop.

Climbing a rope using Prusik loops isn't something you'd do except in emergency. But Prusik loops also have a more everyday use on steep slopes where you can place a rope as a sort of handrail and add Prusik loops to it as an extra security.

THE HARNESS LOOP 🐾

This is a very cunning little dodge for twisting a loop securely into the middle of a piece of rope. In other words, you don't need to manoeuvre the ends of the rope at all.

1 Make an initial circle with the (slightly slack) rope where you want the loop to be. Let's say the rope is coming from the left, circling around anticlockwise and passing *under* the left-hand part.

2 Take the part marked B in the diagram and drag it across the circle to divide it in half.

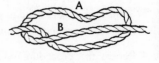

3 Take the part marked A in the diagram, pass it over B and down and out through the bottom part of the hole.

✳ TYING A HORSE ✳

If you go riding in the countryside you'll need to know how to tie your horse when you want to eat your picnic. It needs to be done in such a way that the horse can't pull the knot undone but *you* can.

WARNING

Remember you should *never* tie your horse by its bridle the way they do in cowboy movies. If the horse were to be scared and pull, its mouth could be severely damaged by the bit. A horse should only be tied by a head collar.

1 Pass the free end of the rope over the rail and bring it back underneath.

2 Make a loop on the free part and pass it under the standing part, exactly as for tying a shoe lace.

3 Pull some of the free part through the loop to create a bow and pull the whole thing tight.

If the horse pulls, the knot tightens. However, you can release the knot simply by pulling the free end.

❋ TYING A BOAT ❋

THE CLOVE HITCH 🐾

A boat should be tied to a bollard with a clove hitch, following the same philosophy as tying a horse. The movement of the boat only pulls the knot tighter but it remains easy for you to cast off.

1 Take the free end of the mooring line, pass it around the bollard and under the standing part (the part coming from the boat).

2 Pass the free end round the bollard a second time and jam it by passing it under itself.

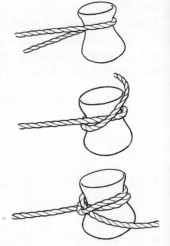

A hitch, by the way, is the name given to any knot that joins a rope to something else. So you can use the clove hitch to tie a rope to a piece of wood, for example. Two other useful hitches are given below.

THE TWO HALF HITCHES

This is a quick and simple hitch that could be used, for example, for attaching a boat fender to a rail.

1 Take a turn around, say, a piece of wood with your rope. Pass the tip of the rope around behind the standing part and then through the loop you've just created.

2 Take the tip round a second time and through the second loop you've just created.

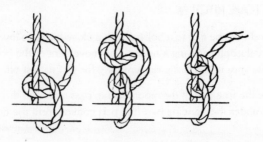

For extra security you can pass the rope twice round the wood before tying the half hitches.

TYING A TENT

THE TAUTLINE HITCH

This is the knot to use when you want to get some tension on a line. Say, for example, the guy rope of a tent.

1 Pass the line around the tent peg anticlockwise and then over and around the standing part twice, *inside* the loop you've created.

2 Pass the tip under and around the standing part, *beyond the knot you just made in Step 1,* and through the new loop you just created.

You'll find you can slide the knot to tighten it but that it will grip under pressure, just like the Prusik knot (above).

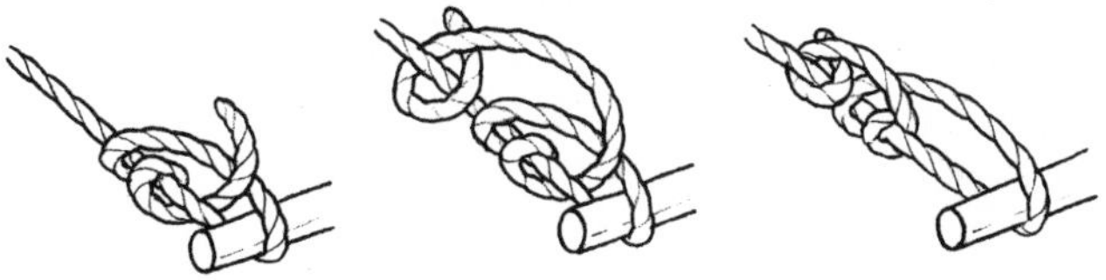

TRACKS AND TRACKING

It's not always easy to see wild animals but the evidence that they exist is all around in the form of tracks in the mud, droppings and feeding signs. With a sharp eye you can put together whole 'stories' of animal behaviour.

❋ TRACKS ❋

All you need to identify tracks are the things you've probably got in your pocket already – a disposable lighter and a few coins (5p, £1 and £2). But bear in mind that animals seldom leave clear tracks. The ground may be too uneven, too hard or too soft and one foot may have landed on the print left by another.

First of all identify the broad category of track:

○ Tracks left by paws *with* 'fingers' and 'toes'
○ Tracks left by paws *without* 'fingers' and 'toes'
○ Tracks left by hooves

TRACKS LEFT BY PAWS WITH 'FINGERS' AND 'TOES'

A few animals have rather human hands and feet, easily recognised by the fact that the marks of the claws are well separated from the main part of the track. In ascending order of size the most commonly encountered tracks are made by a: shrew, wood mouse, mole, vole, dormouse, rat, hedgehog, squirrel, badger, otter. Take out a few coins:

○ The track of the hind foot (longest) can just be covered by a 5p coin. **Shrew** or **wood mouse.**

○ The track of the hind foot (longest) can just be covered by a £1 coin. **Mole** or **vole.**

○ The track of the forefoot (smallest) can just be covered by a 5p coin. **Dormouse** or **rat.**

○ The track of the forefoot (smallest) resembles a human hand and can just be covered by a £2 coin. **Hedgehog.**

○ The track of the hind foot (longest) is narrow and can just be covered by a £1 coin and two 5p coins. **Squirrel.**

○ The track of the forefoot (longest) is the length of a standard disposable lighter and you can put a £1 coin between the imprint of the tip of the claws and the marks left by the nearest pads. **Badger.**

○ The track of the hind foot (longest) is the length of a standard disposable lighter but the imprint of the claws is immediately in front of the pads. **Otter.**

TRACKS LEFT BY PAWS <u>WITHOUT</u> 'FINGERS' OR 'TOES'

In some animals the paws are quite *unlike* human hands or feet having neither 'fingers' nor 'toes' so that the marks of the claws (when present) are immediately in front of the marks left by the pads. In ascending order of size the most commonly encountered tracks are made by a: stoat, weasel, polecat, pine marten, cat, rabbit, wildcat, hare, fox, dog. Take out a few coins:

Pads with four claws. If the track is clear and you can see a triangular main pad plus four other pads with claws then it's a *dog* or a *fox*.

○ **Dog** tracks are round, **fox** tracks are narrow.

◉ **Dog** tracks have blunt claws, **fox** tracks have sharp claws.

◉ **Dog** tracks have the two front claws well separated, **fox** tracks have the two front claws close together.

Pads with five claws. If the track is clear and you can see an elliptical main pad plus five other pads with claws then it's probably a **stoat, weasel, polecat** or **pine marten**.

◉ The track of the forefoot (smallest) isn't quite covered by a £1 coin. **Stoat** or **weasel**.

◉ The track of the forefoot can almost be covered by a £2 coin while the track of the hind foot can be covered by two £1 coins. **Polecat**.

◉ The track of the forefoot can just be covered by a £2 coin and a £1 coin. **Pine marten**.

Pads with four *and* five claws. Rabbits and hares have five toes on their forefeet but only four on the hind feet. The track is roughly oval *without* a central pad.

◉ If the track of the front paw (smallest) can almost be covered by a £2 coin it's a **rabbit**; if it can only be covered by two £2 coins it's a **hare**.

Pads without claws. If the track is clear and you can see pads but no claws then it's a domestic *cat* or a *wildcat*.

◉ **Cat** tracks are the size and shape of a £2 coin.

◉ **Wildcat** tracks are significantly larger than a £2 coin.

TRACKS LEFT BY HOOVES 🐾

If you see tracks left by hoofed animals then, in ascending order of size, they could be from a: muntjac, roe deer, sheep, goat, red deer hind, sika deer, fallow deer, wild boar, red deer stag, cow, horse. With the exception of the horse, all are cloven. Of course, individual animals of the same species will have different hoof sizes so the following is a guide only.

○ The track can just be covered by a £2 coin. **Muntjac.**

○ The track can be covered by a £2 coin and a £1 coin. **Roe deer.**

○ The track can just be covered by two £2 coins and each of the two halves is much narrower at the tip than at the base. **Sheep.**

○ The track can just be covered by two £2 coins and each of the two halves is almost as wide at the tip as at the base. **Goat.**

○ Each half of the track can be covered by two £1 coins and one 5p coin and is shaped like an orange segment with a straight inside edge and a curved outer edge. **Red deer hind.**

○ Each half of the track can be covered by four 5p coins and comes to a sharp point. **Sika deer.**

○ Each half of the track can be covered by three £1 coins and one 5p coin. **Fallow deer.**

○ The track is much wider at the base than at the tip and is composed of four elements – the two parts of the hoof and the two dew claws (the claws on the back of the wild boar's legs). Each half of the hoof can be covered by a £2 coin and a £1 coin, while from the tip to the dew claw can be covered by a standard disposable lighter. **Wild boar.**

- Each half can be covered by a standard disposable lighter. **Red deer stag**.

- A large, almost circular cloven track with no sign of a pad. **Cow**.

- A large, almost circular, non-cloven track with a V-shaped indentation at the back. **Unshod horse**.

- A large, U-shaped track. **Shod horse**.

✳ DROPPINGS ✳

Rule of thumb —○

Herbivores normally produce round droppings which are small relative to the size of the animal.

Carnivores normally produce sausage-shaped droppings with a point at one end.

CYLINDRICAL DROPPINGS

The following are all roughly the length of four £1 coins or a standard disposable lighter (8cm):

- The width of a £2 coin. Black and composed of segments that sometimes come apart, like double-thickness £2 coins pressed together. **Wild boar**.

- The width of a £1 coin. Pointed at one end. Black and containing fur, insect remains and berries. Deposited in open latrines about 4in (10cm) deep. **Badger**.

- Between the width of a £1 coin and a 5p coin. Spirally-twisted point at one end. Light grey to black and containing, fur, feathers, bones, insect chitin and berries. Prominent position. **Fox.**

The length of three £1 coins (6cm). Pointed at one end. Prominent position on rock or tree stump. **Wildcat.** (Note that the wildcat buries its droppings *within* its territory but leaves them uncovered at the boundary as a scent marker.)

The length of three 5p coins (5cm). Black and shiny, containing insect chitin and berries, and deposited at random. **Hedgehog.** (Occasionally the droppings are composed mostly of hair, feathers and bone and are not then shiny-looking).

Can span a £1 coin like a spoke (2cm x 0.5cm). Pale brown. **Brown rat.**

Almost covering a £1 coin (2cm) and just over half as wide (1.3cm). Black with a little point at one end and sometimes a depression at the other. Sometimes in a clump. **Red deer** fewmets.

Spanning a 5p coin (1.5cm x 1cm). Black with a little point at one end and sometimes a depression at the other. Sometimes in a clump. **Fallow deer** fewmets.

Not quite spanning a 5p coin (1.3cm x 0.7cm). Black with a little point at one end and sometimes a depression at the other. Sometimes in a clump. **Roe deer** fewmets.

1cm x 0.3cm. Brown to black. **Black rat** or **Water vole.**

0.6cm x 0.2cm. Brown to black. **House mouse, wood mouse** or **field vole.**

CIGARETTE-SHAPED DROPPINGS

Quite a number of birds leave droppings that resemble the form and contents of a cigarette:

8cm or about the length of a standard disposable lighter. **Goose.**

4cm or about as long as two £1 coins. **Capercaillie.**

2cm or about as long as a £1 coin. **Black grouse** or **Ptarmigan.**

2cm or about as long as a £1 coin; grey-white rather than tobacco-coloured. **Pheasant.**

SPHERICAL DROPPINGS 🌰

About the diameter of a 5p (1.5cm):

○ Pale brown to black and composed of plant matter. **Hare.**

○ Black with flattened faces from being pressed together. **Sheep.**

○ Slightly smaller in diameter than a 5p (about 1cm). Pale brown to black and composed of plant matter. Sometimes found in enormous quantities on slight elevations. **Rabbit.**

✳ PELLETS ✳

Pellets are sometimes confused with droppings but are, in fact, regurgitated from the gizzards of certain birds, including:

○ Members of the gull family
○ The crow family
○ Birds of prey
○ Owls
○ Storks
○ Herons
○ Oystercatchers

They're composed of the indigestible parts of a bird's prey and are found mostly at nesting and roosting sites. They may contain fur, feathers, chitin, bones and shell. Unlike droppings, pellets are not unpleasant to handle – you can happily tease them apart to see what the bird has been eating. Use a magnifying glass to help identify the contents.

Rule of thumb —O

If the pellet contains lots of bone it comes from an owl because the digestive juices of an owl have little effect on bone.

CYLINDRICAL PELLETS

The pellet is the size of a standard disposable lighter (about 8cm x 3cm) and filled with the remains of rodents and other animals and birds, including bones. **Eagle owl.**

The pellet is the length of three £1 coins (6cm x 2cm) and filled with:

O The remains of voles, including bones. **Short-eared owl.**

O Fur and feathers. **Goshawk**

O Fish bones and plant material. **Common gull.**

The pellet is slightly longer than two £1 coins (5 cm x 2 cm):

O Grey, rough, pointed at one or both ends and containing the remains, including bones, of mice and birds up to the size of pigeons. **Tawny owl.**

O Grey, and composed almost entirely of matted fur. **Buzzard.**

O Containing the remains of fish, crabs, snails and molluscs. **Herring gull.**

The pellet is about the length of a £1 coin plus a 5p coin (4cm x 1.5cm):

- Grey, smooth, with rounded ends and containing the remains, including bones, of mice and birds up to the size of pigeons. **Long-eared owl.**

- Grey and containing the remains of mice and small birds, including bones. **Little owl** (autumn/winter).

- Black and containing the remains of beetles together with sand from the digestive tract of worms. **Little owl** (spring/summer).

- Grey and containing mouse fur and small feathers. **Kestrel.**

- Yellowish and containing plant material, insect chitin and small stones. **Crow** family also.

- Dark grey and containing fur and stones. **Crow** family.

- Yellowish or dark and containing fish bones along with plant material. **Black-headed gull.**

- If laid on top of a £2 coin the pellet will just span it (2.5cm x 1cm). It contains mouse fur and small feathers. **Sparrowhawk.**

SPHERICAL OR OVAL PELLETS

About as long and wide as two £1 coins (5cm x 2.5cm). Oval pellet, mostly containing fur but possibly also feathers and insect chitin. **Heron.**

If laid on top of a £2 coin the pellet will just conceal it (3cm diameter). Smooth with a dark grey crust and containing the remains of shrews and mice, including bones. **Barn owl.**

❇ FEEDING SIGNS ❇

CONES 🐾

○ Scales bitten off to leave a frayed tip and frayed central column. Used cones always left in the open. **Squirrel**.

○ Scales bitten off to leave a frayed tip but a very neat central column. Used cones always left in a hidden place. **Mouse**.

○ Scales not bitten off but pulled back to expose the seeds. Used cones always found jammed into a crevice, such as the fissured bark of an oak tree, or discarded underneath. **Woodpecker**.

○ Scales split down the middle to expose the seeds or only slightly in disarray. Used cones found under trees. **Crossbill**.

HAZELNUTS 🐾

○ The shell has been pierced and then cracked apart. **Squirrel**.

○ The shell has a clean hole, as when the top of an egg has been cut off. **Wood mouse**.

○ The shell seems to have been cut in half crossways. **Bank vole**.

○ The shell seems to have been cut in half lengthways with a blunt instrument. **Water vole** or, if there are beak marks, **Woodpecker**.

○ The shell has a tiny hole surrounded by tiny beak marks. **Great tit**.

○ The shell has a large, ragged hole surrounded by beak marks. **Nuthatch**, **Nutcracker** or **Magpie**.

TREES AND BUSHES

- **Shoots** bitten off in a ragged way. **Deer.**
- **Shoots** bitten cleanly through. **Hare and Rabbit.**
- **Bark** torn off in long shreds. **Deer** in summer.
- **Bark** frayed on young trees and side branches broken. **Deer** rubbing the velvet from their antlers (summer/early autumn for red, fallow and sika deer – spring for roe deer).
- **Bark** chiselled off in chunks and clear tooth marks left on the wood:
  - If it's winter and the tooth marks are vertical and high up – **Deer.**
  - If the tooth marks are diagonal – **Sheep** or **Goat.**
  - If the gnawing is only to the bottom 15 cm (the height of two standard disposable lighters) – **Field vole.**
  - If the gnawing is only to the bottom 20 cm (the height of two-and-a-half standard disposable lighters) of *ash trees* – **Water vole.**
  - If the bark has been torn away high up in a tree – **Squirrel.**
  - If the bark has been chipped off anywhere and there are vertical or horizontal beak marks in the wood underneath – **Woodpecker.**

DENS AND SLEEPING PLACES

- Depression – **Deer's** sleeping place.
- A little flower-pot shaped 'tunnel' in long grass – **Hare's** form.
- Spherical mass of twigs and grass close to the trunk of a tree with an entrance hole – **Squirrel's** dray.

○ A hole that can just about be spanned between the out-stretched thumb and little finger of a man's hand (10in/25cm in diameter):

- Usually in a south-facing bank, from which the excavated earth fans out – **Fox's** earth.

- From which the excavated earth has been taken a short distance away – **Badger's** sett.

○ A hole (or series of them) about the diameter of a man's fist (6in/15cm) – **Rabbit's** burrow (usually there will be plenty of droppings for confirmation).

○ A hole that can more or less be spanned by a standard disposable lighter (3in/7.5cm):

- With the excavated soil in a heap outside – **Brown rat's** hole.

- Without a heap of excavated soil outside – **Water vole's** hole.

SOME NESTS

○ Small cup-shaped nest in a little-used postbox, old coat pocket or watering can, if lined with down – **Blue tit.**

○ As above but lined with hair or wool – **Robin.**

○ Cup-shaped, solitary nest of mud clinging under the eaves of a house or barn – **Swallow.**

○ Almost entirely closed mud nest under eaves but usually part of a nesting community – **House martin.**

IDENTIFYING WHAT YOU SEE

✸ WILDLIFE ✸

If you want to identify wildlife without having to lug along half a dozen field guides the best thing is to note down the key features and look them up when you get home. So here's what to make a note of.

BIRDS 🐾

⚙ Size (for example, sparrow-sized or blackbird-sized).

⚙ General colour above and below.

⚙ Any particularly obvious marks or patterns or splodges of colour (try to note where these occur).

⚙ Size and shape of bill, legs, wings, tail and neck.

⚙ Type of walk or flight (such as hops or runs, swoops, soars or hovers).

⚙ Any song or calls.

TREES 🐾

⚙ Size and shape.

⚙ Leaves. Draw the shape. Light green, dark green or grey-green? For needles note whether they grow singly, in pairs or in tufts, on just one side of the twig or all around.

○ Bark – texture and colour.

○ Flowers, fruit and seeds. Are there, for example, cones or catkins or winged seeds?

Here are the identifying features of the seven trees that were mentioned in the chapter on *Fires and cooking* as particularly suitable for firewood:

○ **Ash**: Distinctive black buds; smooth, grey bark becoming fissured in age; notched leaves in pairs on opposite sides of the stem (pinnate); long, narrow brown 'wings' in October.

○ **Beech**: Impressive size; small, rounded catkins on long stalks; pyramidal brown nut inside a tough, shaggy case (the 'mast'); elliptical leaves which are yellow-green in spring; pointed buds; smooth, grey bark.

○ **Birch**: White, scaly bark; oval leaves with pointed tips; plump, drooping, yellow male catkins; shorter female catkins, upright at first; seeds with two papery wings.

○ **Hawthorn**: shrub or small tree with small red fruits (haws) in September; masses of white flowers in May/June; lobed dark-green leaves.

○ **Hornbeam**: dome-shaped tree with smooth, greyish bark; elliptical leaves with prominent veins, pointed tip and jagged edges; short, greenish, feathery catkins; clusters of three-lobed 'wings' in autumn.

○ **Oak**: distinctive, deeply lobed leaves; acorns in autumn; grey bark finely ridged and cracked.

⊛ **Scots Pine**: evergreen with needles in pairs; bark cracked into pinky-coloured plates; small, yellow, male cones in May; female cones are green at first, becoming woody in the third year.

FLOWERS 🌿

⊛ Colour and size.

⊛ Habitat – muddy, brackish, coastal, dunes, grassland, hedgerow, meadow, moor, mountain, riverbank, roadside, rocks, scrub, wasteland.

⊛ Altitude.

⊛ Type of plant – cluster, shrub, grass-like, succulent, semi-succulent, floating.

⊛ Shape of flower – cup, bell, cluster, cone, catkin. Suggest a similarity with a flower you know.

⊛ Petals – irregular (like wild lobelia); two to three (most lilies); four or five (such as buttercup); six to nine (Turk's Cap lily); ten (like daisies), multiple thin petals (such as wild garlic or dandelion); fused petals (such as bindweed).

⊛ Time of year for flowering.

⊛ Arrangement of leaves on the stem.

❋ ANIMALS ❋

Here we've selected some of nature's most confusable animals and given hints on how to tell them apart.

RABBIT OR HARE? 🐾

○ If it has extremely long back legs and is bounding then it's a hare.

○ If it's moving in small hops then it's probably a rabbit.

○ Seen side by side hares are larger with longer ears than rabbits.

Rule of thumb ─○

If there's more than one of them then they're rabbits; hares tend to be solitary except at mating time.

MOLE, VOLE OR SHREW? 🐾

Actually you'll be lucky to actually lay eyes on any of these chaps as they're highly secretive.

○ Highly visible surface tunnels mean voles. They're so shallow you can sometimes see the occupant moving along under a thin layer of soil. *But* shrews sometimes inhabit vole (and mole) burrows.

○ Voles create motorways – visible paths about two inches wide caused by their constant traffic.

○ Moles tend to construct much deeper then voles (although their access tunnels can be quite close to the surface) and create their distinctive molehills.

○ Voles resemble mice; shrews have extremely pointed noses; moles have spade-shaped front feet and dense, short velvet-like fur.

WEASEL , STOAT, ERMINE, POLECAT, AMERICAN MINK, PINE MARTEN OR FERRET? 🐾

These long, thin creatures are easily confused. In fact, all of them, with the exception of the pine marten (*Martes martes*) are members of *Mustela* family.

⊙ The **pine marten** (upland Scotland, Northern England and Wales) is the largest of the group at 900g -2000g. If you see something that resembles a small fox up a tree then it's a pine marten. Chestnut-coloured, it has a cream or yellow chin and chest patch and an extremely bushy tail. An excellent tree climber.

⊙ Next in size is the **polecat** at 600g-1500g. At the beginning of the 20th century it was extinct in Britain except Wales but numbers are now slowly increasing. At a glance it's easily told from the pine marten and the others in this section by a 'face mask' of white around the nose, above the eyes and on the tips of the ears against a background of dark brown or black fur. On the body the yellowish underfur sometimes shows through the dark brown. Generally active at dusk, dawn and during the night.

⊙ The **American mink**, third in size at 600g-1000g, is quickly distinguished by being the only animal in the group that, at a glance, seems to be a uniform dark brown all over. Only close up is it possible to see a little white on the chin. The British population stems from escaped farmed animals and is now widespread except in the mountains. Almost always seen close to water, usually a river, and active day and night.

⊙ The **stoat** (150g-300g) is roughly the size of a squirrel but with a slender stretched-out body and a shorter, far less bushy tail. In its summer coat of brown above and yellowish-white below it could be confused with the weasel but the black tip to the tail is always distinctive. In winter it can be white (but still with the black-tipped tail) when it's known as the *ermine* and could then be confused with feral ferrets.

- The **weasel** (40g-170g) resembles the summer-coated stoat but is generally smaller and, unlike the stoat, has only a short tail without a black tip. Widespread all over Great Britain.

- The **ferret** is the domesticated polecat but is white, cream or light brown and therefore without the black and white 'face mask.' However, there are some feral populations as well as ferret/polecat hybrids.

MINK OR OTTER?

- If it has a body and tail about the size of a fox then it's an otter; a mink is half the size or less of an otter and only a fifth to a tenth of the weight.

- If the head looks too small for the body it's a mink.

- If it has a bushy tail it's a dry mink; the otter's tail is never bushy.

- If you see it eating what it's caught it's probably an otter; a mink takes its catch back home.

- If it runs away on land it's probably a mink; if it heads straight for the water it's probably an otter.

MOUSE OR SHREW?

You're most likely to see these when the cat makes you a present of them. The shrew is the one the cat *doesn't* eat (because there's a scent gland which puts Felix off).

○ **Colour** – the house mouse is greyish brown; the wood/field mouse is a warm rust; the water shrew is charcoal grey above and silver under; the common shrew is ochre above and paler under; the pygmy shrew is grey-brown above and paler under.

○ **Ears** – mice have large ears, shrews have small ears.

○ **Eyes** – mice have large eyes, shrews have small eyes.

○ **Nose** – mice have relatively rounded noses, shrews' faces all draw out into a long point.

○ **Size** – shrews are typically half the weight and size of mice.

FROG OR TOAD?

You wouldn't probably choose to kiss either but so you don't get it wrong:

○ **Skin** – frogs are slimy and smooth; toads are dry and warty.

○ **Legs** – frogs have long back legs, toads have short ones.

○ **Eggs** – frogs lay in clusters, toads lay in chains.

LIZARD OR NEWT?

○ **Skin** – lizards have scaly skin; newts have velvety skin.

○ **Tail** – lizards have snake-like tails; newts have flat, rudder-like tails.

○ **Breeding** – common lizards normally have live young; sand lizards lay eggs in a shallow pit; newts wrap their eggs in pond vegetation.

BUTTERFLY OR MOTH? 🔍

- Most butterflies fly during the day whereas moths usually fly at night.

- Butterflies always have little knobs on the ends of their antennae but moths have little feathery tendrils or nothing.

- Most butterflies have slim hairless bodies while most moths have rounder furry abdomens.

Rule of thumb —O

Most butterflies rest with their wings held together above their bodies but moths tend to rest with their wings flat out.

OH DEER! RED, ROE, FALLOW, MUNTJAC, SIKA OR CHINESE? 🔍

There are six species of deer to be found in Britain, the Red, Roe, Fallow, Muntjac, Sika and Chinese water deer. Only the first two are true natives and the fallow was reintroduced long ago, possibly by the Romans. In descending order of size:

Red

- Big. With full antlers can stand as tall as a man.

- Beefy. The largest mammal in Britain, it can reach up to 400lb (180kg) in the south but only slightly more than half that in the harsher climes of Scotland.

- Dark red or brown in summer. More grey-brown in winter. Cream underbelly and yellowish rump patch bisected by short tail.

○ Antlers can be huge and multi-pointed.

○ Usually in single sex herds.

Fallow

○ Up to three feet high (1m).

○ Males about 150lb-300lb (70kg-140kg).

○ Warm-brown summer coat with white spots on back and flanks; dark, grey-brown winter coat without spots.

○ Bright white rump almost invariably cut through by a dark tail.

○ Antlers are flat 'palms' from which tines stick out.

○ Usually found in herds.

Sika

○ Up to three feet high (1m).

○ Can weigh around 200lb (90kg) in rich food areas, though in the Scottish Highlands they are more normally around 100lb (45kg).

○ Red-brown with spots, sika are easily confused with fallow deer but there is almost always a pronounced black dorsal stripe and the antlers are different.

○ White rump patch like fallow deer but tail cutting through it is slightly less noticeable.

○ Antlers completely unlike flat 'palms' of fallow deer and more like those of red deer.

○ Live in herds.

- Can emit a quite startling scream during the rut.

Roe

- Not normally much over two feet high (66cm).

- Males slightly heavier than females but only about 55lb (25kg).

- Fox-red in summer, grey-brown in winter.

- Creamy-white rump patch with a hardly noticeable tail. The female has a little tuft of hair at the bottom of the patch.

- Short antlers with a maximum of six points.

- Usually in small family groups or solitary.

Muntjac

- Small. Usually under two feet tall (66cm).

- Slender. Not normally weighing more than 35lb (16kg).

- Warm-brown in summer, more grey in winter. The long tails are hairy and gingery brown on the upper-side but white underneath. When the Muntjac is alarmed the tail is raised.

- Short antler spikes, raked back.

- Mature bucks (males) have small tusks but not as visible as for Chinese water deer.

- Live singly or in small family groups.

- Known as the 'barking deer' because it can bark repeatedly at four to six second intervals.

Chinese water deer

○ Small. Usually under two feet tall (66cm).

○ Look chunkier than their average 30lb (14kg) weight suggests with a head that looks too small for the body.

○ Red-brown and sleek in summer but in winter sandy-brown and shaggy, especially around the head.

○ No antlers but the males have very visible tusks.

○ No rump patch.

○ Will bounce away when startled.

○ Live singly or in pairs.

TIP ❦

Only male deer have antlers and they cast and regrow them every year, so that for part of the year they can look like large females.

GREY SEAL OR COMMON/HARBOUR SEAL? 🦭

There are two species of seal living around the UK, the grey seal and the smaller common or harbour seal:

○ Size. Grey seals are generally 6ft-9ft long (2m-3m approx) and weigh up to 650lb (300kg). Common seals, on the other hand, are up to 6ft (2m approx) and weigh a maximum of around 220lb (100kg).

○ Faces. Grey seals have an elongated muzzle whereas common seals are more 'pug-like' with a short snout.

- **Colour**. Grey to brown in both species.

- **Habitat**. Grey seals *prefer* rocky coasts and common seals *prefer* sandy coasts.

- **Behaviour**. Grey seals tend to come ashore *only* for the mating season in October/November; common seals mate ashore in June/July but also like to sunbathe on sandbanks at other times.

- **Young**. Grey seal pups are born with a white coat, which lasts about two weeks, and stay out of the water for between three and four weeks. Common seal pups get into the water within an hour of birth.

❋ ROCKS ❋

To identify rocks you'll need a good magnifying glass and a small penknife to scrape away the weathering layer (usually a thin crust of carbonate of lime) so you can see what it's really made of. A visit to the geology department of the local museum will be a big help. Any rock, boulder or pebble that you want to identify will fall into one of three main classifications: sedimentary, igneous or metamorphic.

IDENTIFYING SEDIMENTARY ROCKS

As the name suggests, sedimentary rock is formed from sediments compacted together. These sediments may come from:

- The weathering of other rocks.
- Plants and animals.
- By evaporation, leading to the precipitation of salts.

Rules of thumb —○

○ If a rock contains fossils it is *definitely* sedimentary.

○ If a rock shows bedding (layers) it is *probably* sedimentary (but certain igneous rocks also show bedding).

Shale

Shale is the commonest sedimentary rock, making up 70 per cent of all sedimentary rocks in the Earth's crust.

○ Black, grey, brown, red, dark green, dark blue or off-white.
○ Fine grain (difficult to see with the naked eye).
○ Smells of wet mud when damp.
○ Powders when scratched.
○ Splits into fine layers.

Sandstone

Sandstone is the second most common sedimentary rock. Strength varies according to whether or not the individual grains are 'cemented' together.

○ Wide variety of colours.
○ Composed mainly of sand-sized grains up to 0.08in (2mm) in diameter.
○ Bedding (layers) usually apparent.
○ Can scrape off grains with a sharp point.

Limestone

○ Limestone is not always white but can be yellow, brown, red or even black.
○ Texture varies from fine to coarse.

- Can contain fossils.
- Easily scratched.
- Effervesces with dilute hydrochloric acid.

Chalk

- A pure form of limestone.
- White, grey or yellow.
- Fine-grained.
- Porous.
- Crumbles easily.
- Easily scratched.
- Effervesces with dilute hydrochloric acid.

Coal *(including peat, anthracite, lignite and bituminous coal)*

- Light brown through to black.

- Peat is felt-like and soft; lignite is like dried, woody peat;
  bituminous coals have layers which can contain visible plant
  matter or fossils and break easily into rectangular pieces;
  anthracite is shiny.

IDENTIFYING IGNEOUS ROCKS

Igneous rocks are either glassy or crystalline and are produced from
hot magma rising from the lower crust or upper mantle of the
Earth.

Pumice

- Usually grey or yellowish.
- No visible crystals.
- No layers.

- Extremely porous with lots of vesicles (holes).
- Extremely light.
- Makes spherical to egg-shaped pebbles.

Granite

- White, grey, or pink.
- Coarse grains.
- Can contain crystals.
- Hard.
- Very difficult to break.
- Makes spherical to egg-shaped pebbles.

Basalt

- Dark grey to black (but can develop a greenish or reddish crust).
- Fine grains.
- Can contain crystals.
- Can have gas bubbles.
- Difficult to break.
- Can split into spectacular column shapes such as seen at the Devil's Causeway in Northern Ireland.
- Makes spherical to egg-shaped pebbles.

IDENTIFYING METAMORPHIC ROCKS

Metamorphic rocks are those that have been altered under high temperature or pressure.

Slate

- Was clay or shale.
- Mostly grey to black but can be red, purple or green.

- Fine grains.
- Thin, smooth layers.
- Splits easily.
- Can scratch glass.

Marble

- Was limestone.
- Pure white, grey or light brown often streaked with yellow, brown, blue, green, red or black.
- Visible crystals often in mosaic-like patterns.
- Soft (won't scratch glass).
- Makes spherical pebbles.

Schist

- Various colours including green, blue, brown and black.
- Minerals easily seen by eye or lens.
- Needle-like grains or platy minerals lie with their long directions parallel.
- Splits quite easily into layers.

Gneiss

- Commonly white, pink or grey bands.
- Medium to coarse grained.
- Has clear ribbon-like layers.
- Has clear crystals in bands, often alternating light and dark.
- Very hard.
- Can sparkle when wet.
- Makes round to oval pebbles.

Quartzite

- Was sandstone.

- White, grey, pink or red.
- Can be noticeably lustrous.
- Resembles marble but is much harder and doesn't react with dilute hydrochloric acid; brittle.
- Makes spherical to oval pebbles.
- Will flash orange and give off a noticeable smell when two pebbles are struck together (even under water).

FOSSILS 🦴

Most fossils are the rock-like copies of the hard parts (bones, teeth, shells or coral) of creatures which existed between 10,000 and several million (possibly billion) years ago. Occasionally you can also find fossilised footprints, eggs, droppings and plants.

Fossils are normally found in sedimentary rocks because they can't survive the heat or pressure that creates metamorphic rocks or the heat of the magma from which igneous rocks are formed. But very occasionally you will find fossils in rocks formed from rapidly cooling volcanic ash.

The process is:

- Death (the soft parts usually get eaten quite quickly).

- Deposition. The object is covered and protected with layers of sand and silt.

- Permineralisation. Chemicals in the object change as it decays. Rocky minerals (calcite, iron or silica) replace the original form. The object is now actually rock.

- Erosion. Time and weather expose the object.

Where to look for fossils

Look for fossils:

○ Mainly in limestone, chalk and shale.

○ In areas where there has been a major uplifting of rock or a
large amount of erosion, such as:

– Mountains
– Cliffs
– Bluffs
– Canyons
– River-banks

And, with permission:

○ Fields
○ Quarries
○ Spoil heaps
○ Constructions sites

Good fossil-finding areas in the UK include:

○ East Cliff, Whitby, Yorkshire
○ Lyme Bay, Dorset
○ Pembroke Coast, Wales
○ Isle of Wight
○ Hastings
○ The Cotswolds

Some common fossils

These are some of the fossils you're most likely to see:

○ **Graptolites** were very simple marine creature shaped like
horny rods. The fossil looks something like a saw blade.

○ **Trilobite**. Three-lobed crustaceans that were the forerunners of today's lobsters, crabs and prawns, the fossil resembles a wood louse.

○ **Brachiopods** were bivalve shellfish like today's clams, oysters and mussels. The commonest form resembles a cockle.

○ **Crinoid** fossils look a little like very fine corrugated tubing as used for electric cables. Some limestone is packed with them to such an extent it is known as crinoidal limestone.

○ **Ammonites** are perhaps the best-known fossil, having the spectacular shape of a ram's horn.

○ **Belemnites** can often be found wherever you find ammonites. Related to today's cuttlefish, the fossilised back shell of these long extinct ten-legged creatures is what you'll see. Look for elongated cylindrical bullet-shapes.

Semi-precious stones

As these are mostly found on beaches in the UK they're included in the chapter on *Coastline*. See pages 98–101.

THE NIGHT SKY

Watching the night sky clear of light pollution is one of the great joys of camping in the countryside.

THE STARS

A complete rotation of the stars takes 23 hours 56 minutes which means any star will be four minutes earlier each night or around two hours a month. In a year, therefore, the constellations will, rather conveniently, return to their original 'starting positions'.

THE PLOUGH OR BIG DIPPER OR CHARLES'S WAIN

These seven bright stars in the constellation of Ursa Major never set in the British night sky (although they might be obscured by buildings and hills when they're close to the horizon). By the way, they're about one thousand million light years from Earth – that's to say, you're seeing them as they were one thousand million years ago.

The seven stars form a very distinctive shape that is actually more like a pot with a slightly bent handle. Once you know it you'll always spot it and it's the key to finding lots of other stars and constellations. For example, the two stars furthest from the handle are called Merak and – the very last – Dubhe. A line drawn from Merak to Dubhe and continued on into space would come very close to the Pole Star (see below).

POLARIS OR THE POLE STAR 🐾

The Pole Star might be considered the most important star because it more or less indicates north. At night, therefore, you can use it for navigation. In order to identify it, first find the Plough (see above). If you're still not quite positive which it is, it's the last star of the constellation known as the Little Bear or Ursa Minor. The Little Bear actually looks more like a kite, with four stars forming a diamond-shape and a 'tail' of three more stars. The Pole Star is the last one in the tail. Unfortunately, the Little Bear is only visible on a very clear night well away from light pollution.

ORION 🐾

Orion is the most brilliant star group in the night sky. It rises in the east and sets in the west. The easiest way to find it is to look out for the three bright stars that form 'Orion's belt'. They're close together and in an almost perfectly straight line. When you've once identified the 'belt' you'll never forget it. Above the belt to the left is the star Betelgeuse which has a reddish tinge. Below to the right is the star Rigel which has a very hard, blue-white light.

Immediately under the 'belt', as if hanging from it, is a faint pattern of stars known as 'Orion's sword'. The central, fuzzy-looking light in the sword is actually the Orion Nebula, one of the most exciting things in the sky because it's the nearest star-forming region to Earth.

THE PLEIADES 🐾

The Pleiades is the tightest visible huddle of stars in the night sky. Follow the line of Orion's Belt (see above) up to the west and there it is. Six can be picked out with the naked eye and they almost seem to touch.

ALDEBARAN 🐾

The brilliant red star half way between Orion's belt and the Pleiades is known as Aldebaran.

SIRIUS OR THE DOG STAR 🐾

Sirius is the brightest star in northern skies, partly because, as we now know, it's actually two stars known as Sirius A and Sirius B. It's also one of the nearest to Earth. You can find it by following the line of the three stars of Orion's Belt downwards to the east. It's in the constellation known as The Great Dog or Canis Major and shines with a strong greenish light near the southern horizon in winter.

TIP 🐾

The brightness or 'magnitude' of stars is rated on a scale which gives the highest number to the dimmest. To complicate matters, some objects are so bright they're given minus numbers. Thus the sun is –26.7 and Sirius is –1.5. On a clear, moonless night away from light pollution the human eye can pick out a magnitude of 6.

ARCTURUS 🐾

The handle of The Plough (see above) points to a constellation known as The Herdsman, and just beyond it to a little semi-circle of stars known as the Corona Borealis or The Northern Crown. Arcturus, the bottom star of The Herdsman, is a brilliant reddish-yellow, and the third brightest star in the northern hemisphere.

THE MILKY WAY 🐌

The Milky Way, which appears as a luminous band across the heavens, is in fact the galaxy of which Earth is itself a part. In other words, we're actually inside the Milky Way and the galactic centre is a mere 26,000 light years away. The Milky Way's several billion stars would be an even more impressive spectacle if it were not for the dust clouds that obscure much of it. If we could see the Milky Way from far out in space it would appear as a beautiful spiral, something like a Catherine wheel.

❋ THE PLANETS ❋

Planets are satellites of the sun, just as the Earth is. They revolve in regular orbits around the sun but, relative to the stars, their positions are irregular, which makes them rather difficult to spot. Their identifying characteristic is a steady radiance (in contrast to the 'twinkling' of stars).

Rule of thumb ⟜○

The path of the sun is known as the *ecliptic*. To narrow down your search for the planets it helps to know that they, and the moon, follow the same general line in a band either side of the ecliptic known as the Zodiac.

TIPS 🐾

○ To find the position of the planets for any given day and time you'll have to consult an Astronomical Almanac.

○ A pair of binoculars will make a big difference. The performance of binoculars is described by two numbers such as 6 x 30 or 7 x 50. The first number is the magnification and the second number is the size of the objective lens in millimetres. The larger the objective the better for night viewing.

VENUS 🔭

Venus is the third brightest object in the sky after the sun and moon with a magnitude of –4 and, therefore, the easiest of the planets to spot. However, (as with Mercury) it's only visible at morning or evening twilight. Like the moon it appears to go through phases and, through a telescope, is sometimes seen as a crescent. It's of similar size to the Earth but has a surface temperature of almost 500°C, so no chance of going to live there.

MERCURY 🔭

Like Venus, Mercury is only visible at morning or evening twilight. Mariner 10, the first spacecraft to fly by in 1974, showed it to be inhospitably pitted with thousands of impact craters.

JUPITER 🔭

Jupiter is the largest planet and 318 times more massive than the Earth. It glows with a yellow light although, seen from a spacecraft, it seems more like pink marble. The famous 'Great Red Spot' was discovered by the French astronomer Gian Cassini in 1665 using a primitive telescope. It's now known to be a storm several thousand miles across, already lasting some 350 years or more and with winds of 180mph.

SATURN 🔭

At 95 times more massive than Earth, Saturn is considered by many to be the most beautiful planet on account of its extra-ordinary rings which are made of hydrogen.

It has a steady yellow radiance.

MARS 🐾

Mars, known as 'The Red Planet' because it glows with a reddish light, is man's best hope of creating another inhabitable planet in our solar system. A Martian day is conveniently only just over half an hour longer than our own although a Martian year is almost two Earth years. There are polar ice caps, there's water and there are seasons but, unfortunately, the mean temperature is a chilly –23°C.

URANUS, NEPTUNE AND PLUTO 🐾

These three planets (or two, technically, as Pluto is now classified as a dwarf planet) are invisible to the naked eye.

MAN-MADE LANDSCAPE

There are still parts of Britain in which you may fondly imagine you're strolling through wilderness but, in fact, all of the landscape has been altered by human activity. Here are some of the things to look out for.

�֎ HEDGES ✷

In Britain there are records of hedges more or less as we know them today going back to the Roman era. In Anglo-Saxon times hedges all over Britain were mentioned in the Magna Carta. Hedging increased rapidly in the time of the 'Great Enclosures' (mid-1800s CE to the mid-1900s CE) and then suffered serious decline from the end of the Second World War until in 1997 a government study was launched to protect important hedgerows.

❂ It is now forbidden to remove or damage most of Britain's hedgerows without permission from the local planning authority.

Although hedges are thought of as quintessentially English there are also hedges a-plenty through Western France, Northern Italy, Austria and Greece.

DATING HEDGEROWS 🐚

According to *Hooper's Rule* the number of species in a hedge is roughly equal to the age of the hedge in centuries:

○ Measure out 30 good paces along the hedge.

○ Count the different species, excluding under-shrubs such as ivy or blackberry.

○ Don't differentiate between different species of the same family – that is to say an oak is an oak, a beech a beech.

○ For each species count 100 years.

In Britain the most usual trees and shrubs noted for hedge-dating are listed below. But you don't actually have to be able to identify them. All you have to be able to see is how many different kinds of trees and shrubs there are.

○ Alder, Apple (including crab-apple), Ash, Beech, Blackthorn, Broom, Buckthorn, Cherry, Cherry-Plum, Dogwood, Elder, Elm, Furze, Guelder-Rose, Hawthorn, Hazel, Holly, Hornbeam, Lime, Maple, Oak, Pine, Plum, Poplar, Privet, Rowan, Sallow, Service, Spindle, Sycamore, Wayfaring-Tree, Whitebeam, Willow, Yew.

✳ HOLES ✳

An unexplained hole, pond or dell in the ground might have been made by a meteor, a glacier, a man with a spade, a JCB – or the fairies. Here are some clues:

○ **If the hole is man-made and dug for the contents** there will be an obvious lack of nearby spoil (or, at any rate, insufficient to fill the hole); there should be some sign of a track leading to and from the hole and perhaps a ramp into the area.

○ **If the hole is man-made but not dug for the contents** the spoil will be dumped close by as bumps or hillocks, perhaps disguised by plants. Such depressions might have been:

- Boles, or shallow depressions scooped out for smelting by lead miners in the hills of the Peak District.
- Charcoal burning pits.
- Corn-kilns, made for drying grain in the damp conditions in the Highlands, the Western Isles and Ireland; the pits were lined with stone and thatched over.
- Fishponds – in the Middle Ages a pond beside the manor or castle was the equivalent of today's freezer.
- Saw pits.

○ **Are the edges of the pit or depression rounded or sharp?**
Anything with sharp edges is likely to be man-made, while rounded contours suggest something natural. Natural causes include:
- 'Kettle-holes' from glaciation
- Sinkholes in the underlying chalk

�֎ LUMPS �֎

Anywhere you see a solitary lump, bump or hump in the English landscape (especially if it's near a long-established population centre) you're probably looking at an ancient *barrow* (burial place) or a fortification (unless it's a glacial feature, see below).

BARROWS 🐾

English place names ending with -bury, -borough or -bourg come from the ancient word *beorg* meaning barrow. Other names for barrow include:

○ Cairn
○ Carn
○ Kurgan
○ Tumulus

These burial places come in all shapes and sizes and, excavated or not, are protected under the UK Ancient Monuments and Archaeological Areas Act.

Burial places of this kind were in use all over Europe from about 5,000 years ago. Artefacts provide the most reliable form of dating but size and shape can provide a rough guide:

◉ **Long.** *Long barrows* date from around 3000 BCE to 2000 BCE. They're mostly found in Dorset, Wiltshire, Hampshire, Sussex, Yorkshire and Lincolnshire. Can be extremely large. The biggest in Britain is the East Kennet Long Barrow near Marlborough, Wiltshire, measuring 350ft (105m) x 100ft (30m) x 20ft (6m) high. But the nearby West Kennet burial site is only slightly smaller and can be visited. During excavation (in the 19th and mid-20th centuries) the remains of 50 people of various age groups were found.

◉ **Oval.** Oval barrows may have been a transitional stage between long and rounded barrows. The Gallows Barrow near Amesbury, also in Wiltshire, is a good example, dating from around 2400 BCE and measuring 75ft (22.5m) x 50ft (15m).

◉ **Round.** Smaller round barrows seem to have been introduced by immigrants during the Bronze Age, although larger round barrows had already been constructed. Generally these smaller barrows date from 2000 BCE to1000 BCE. Some have ditches around them or earth/stone banks. The bell shape is a variation.

◉ **Square.** Generally date from around 800 BCE to 43 CE. Contained valuable items such as spears for the men and mirrors for the women.

◉ **Dolmens** are burial chambers made of large, flat stones stood on edge with another flat stone horizontally on top as a roof.

Normally they would have been covered with earth to create barrows but many have now been uncovered to stand alone and a few were never covered in the first place. A good example is Wayland's Smithy in Oxfordshire.

FORTIFICATIONS 🐚

○ **Crannogs** are artificial islands made in lakes in Scotland and Ireland for defensive purposes.

○ **Motte-and-bailey fortresses** were introduced by the Normans and consisted of a roughly oval ditch with an earth rampart behind and, in one corner, a 'crème caramel' shaped mound (the motte) anything up to 40ft (12m) high.

○ **Rampart farmsteads** date from around the 6th century BCE and consist of ditches and earth or stone ramparts encircling the top of a hill or cutting across a small headland.

○ **Ringforts or raths** were circular rampart farmsteads built in Ireland until as recently as 1000 CE. Some 30,000 still survive.

○ **Roman forts** can be distinguished from rampart farmsteads by their regular shape. They were normally rectangular with rounded corners and on top of the surviving ditch and earth rampart there would have been a wooden palisade.

HORSESHOE-SHAPED MOUNDS 🐚

Beside streams, these have nothing to do with burials or fortifications but are known as 'deer roasts'. They were places used for the preparation of carcasses, involving a hearth and a pit in which water was heated with stones from the fire.

✳ DYKES ✳

Dykes are trenches with accompanying ridges and were used as fences, boundary markers and fortifications from pre-Roman times. One of the most famous examples is the 120-mile Offa's Dyke, built by King Offa in the 8th century CE to keep the Welsh and Mercians apart. But they were also used for drainage, as in Romney Marsh and the Fens.

❊ RIDGE AND FURROW ❊

If you see a field with a strange undulating appearance it's a sure sign of the medieval strip field system. Typically each strip or ridge would have been 11yards (8m) wide, 220 yards (200m) long and divided from the next by a ditch or furrow. It's from this that comes the furlong – a furrow long. The average farmer would have worked around 70 ridges amounting to some 20 acres in total.

❊ GLACIAL LANDSCAPE ❊

Many of the lumps and holes you see around you are man-made, but not all. Places such as the Lake District and Scotland have plenty of glacial features.Although the last Ice Age in Britain ended about 20,000 years ago it's left plenty of signs of its presence. And some of them, like kettle holes, moraines and drumlins, can seem to be man-made.

Arete
A scarily-sharp ridge formed by the creation of a corrie (see below) each side of a mountain.

Corrie (or Cirque)
Huge, armchair-shaped scoop in the side of a mountain, created by ice.

Drumlin

Drumlins are small hills, often grouped close together, and distinctively shaped like half-eggs cut through lengthwise. They're caused by a glacier piling up mounds of stone and clay against an obstacle, so that the debris gradually tapers away as the glacier moves. The thinner end of a drumlin always points in the direction the glacier was travelling in.

Hanging Valley

Imagine a broken gutter from which the water cascades down the sheer wall of a house. That's roughly the idea of a hanging valley. They're created when a small side glacier is cut off by the passing of the mother glacier. After the ice has melted the side valley 'hangs' spectacularly far above the main valley floor.

Kettle Holes

As glaciers retreat some areas of ice prove more resistant and debris builds up around them. When those blocks of ice melt in their turn, the debris is left as a raised area and the space left in the middle is a kettle hole.

Moraine

Stony junk (from boulders to grit) left by the passage of the glacier. Mounds of it left at the side of a valley are known as *lateral* while if the mound marks the end of the glacier it's known as *terminal*.

Pyramidal Peak (or Horn)

An impressively sharp mountain peak carved by the formation of three or more corries.

U-shaped Valleys

A valley which would have started life as a V-shape, formed by river erosion, but later scoured into a U by ice.

EMERGENCY NUMBERS

The principal emergency number, not just for police, fire brigade and ambulance but also for coastguards, mountain rescue and cave rescue, is, of course:

999 🕿

You can also dial the EU emergency number. It should work even on a mobile phone which is out of range for normal calls:

112 🕿

If you need advice on the treatment of an injury phone NHS Direct:

0845 4647 🕿

✣ OTHER USEFUL CONTACTS ✣

WEATHER 🕿

Online weather forecasts are available at:
www.metoffice.gov.uk

Mountain area forecasts can be obtained by phoning:
0870 900 0100

Weather reports can be delivered to your mobile phone for 25p plus your normal text charges:

○ Text WC TODAY plus the name of the town/area and send to 83141.

○ For a 5-day forecast text WC 5DAY plus the name of the town/area and send to 83141.

Longer and more detailed MMS (multimedia messaging service) forecasts can be delivered to your mobile phone for £1 plus your normal text charges:

○ Text WC MMS plus the name of the town/area and send to 83141.

TIDAL PREDICTIONS 🦶

Telephone 0151 795 4800 or see **www.pol.ac.uk/ntslf/tides**

USEFUL CONTACTS 🖋

You'll find all the websites referred to in this book on our website at www.whiteladderpress.com to make it easier for you to access them. Click on 'Useful contacts' next to the information about this book.

CONTACT US 🖋

You're welcome to contact White Ladder Press if you have any questions or comments for either us or the authors. Please use whichever of the following routes suits you.

Phone: **0208 334 1600**

Email: **enquiries@whiteladderpress.com**

Fax: **0208 334 1601**

Address: **2nd Floor, Westminster House, Kew Road, Richmond, Surrey TW9 2ND**

Website: **www.whiteladderpress.com**

WHAT CAN OUR WEBSITE DO FOR YOU? 🖋

If you want more information about any of our books, you'll find it at www.whiteladderpress.com. In particular you'll find extracts from each of our books, and reviews of those that are already published. We also run special offers on future titles if you order online before publication. And you can request a copy of our free catalogue.

Many of our books have links pages, useful addresses and so on relevant to the subject of the book. You'll also find out a bit more about us and, if you're a writer yourself, you'll find our submission guidelines for authors. So please check us out and let us know if you have any comments, questions or suggestions.

INDEX